Library of
Davidson College

Perspectives in American History

No. 19
THE DEVELOPMENT OF METHODISM
IN THE OLD SOUTHWEST, 1783-1824

THE DEVELOPMENT OF METHODISM
IN THE OLD SOUTHWEST

1783-1824

BY

WALTER BROWNLOW POSEY

PROFESSOR OF HISTORY IN BIRMINGHAM-SOUTHERN COLLEGE

PORCUPINE PRESS
Philadelphia 1974

Library of Congress Cataloging in Publication Data

Posey, Walter Brownlow, 1900-
   The development of Methodism in the old Southwest, 1783-1824.

   (Perspectives in American history, no. 19)
   Reprint of the 1933 ed. published by Weatherford Print. Co., Tuscaloosa, Ala.
     Bibliography: p.
     1. Methodist Church in the Old Southwest--History. I. Title. II. Series: Perspectives in American history (Philadelphia), no. 19.
BX8241.P67   1974   287'.676   73-18408
ISBN 0-87991-339-8

First edition 1933
(Tuscaloosa, Alabama: Weatherford Printing Co., 1933)

Reprinted 1974 by
PORCUPINE PRESS, INC.
1317 Filbert St.
Philadelphia, Pennsylvania 19107

Manufactured in the United States of America

*To the Memory of
My Mother*

The whole country is under a debt of gratitude to the Methodist circuit riders, the Methodist pioneer preachers, whose movement westward kept pace with the movement of the frontier, who shared all the hardships in the life of the frontiersman, while at the same time ministering to that frontiersman's spiritual needs and seeing that his pressing material cares and the hard and grinding poverty of his life did not wholly extinguish the divine fire within his soul.

THEODORE ROOSEVELT.

PREFACE

The influence of religious groups in Western life has indeed been so large that it seems remarkable that church history has failed to keep step with the political and social history of America. Within recent years there have appeared several studies of frontier churches, but the subject yet lies undisturbed below the surface.

This book traces the development in the Old Southwest of the Methodist Episcopal Church from 1783, when it first appeared west of the Alleghenies, until 1824, when it may be considered to have assumed definite shape. By this time the organization of the church had reached approximately the same form which it has today. To have continued the study beyond 1824 would have introduced no new phases of structure other than the adjustment of expansion into more distant regions.

Some articles and portions of articles previously published in the *Mississippi Valley Historical Review, Tennessee Historical Magazine, Social Science,* and *Nashville Christian Advocate* have been brought together in this book, and for permission to use them again I am indebted to the editors of these journals.

The suggestion of this study and the pleasure of inspiration came from the late Walter L. Fleming, an affectionate student of Southern life. For innumerable criticisms and guidance I owe much to Dr. William C. Binkley, of Vanderbilt University, whose scholarship and critical acumen have been invaluable. For reading and criticizing the manuscript I am indebted to Dr. Carl S. Driver and Dr. Frank L. Owsley of Vanderbilt University; Dr. Arthur P. Whitaker of Cornell University; Dr. William W. Sweet of the University of Chicago. To my friend and colleague, Professor Wilbur D. Perry, of Birmingham-Southern College, I am grateful for commas and colons. Justice demands an expression of indebtedness to my wife who has read and helped to revise the manuscript.

WALTER BROWNLOW POSEY.

CONTENTS

	Page
Preface	XI

Chapter
		Page
I	Methodism Crosses the Alleghenies, 1783-1799	1
II	The Period of the Camp Meeting, 1800-1811	17
III	The Circuit Rider Among Frontier Folk	35
IV	Earthquakes and War, 1812-1815	48
V	Educational Efforts and Achievements	62
VI	Missionary Efforts Among the Indians	81
VII	The Negro and the Methodist Church	91
VIII	Efforts for a Temperate Social Order	100
IX	The Organic Structure of the Church	112
X	Methodism Reaches Maturity	123
	Bibliography	130

THE DEVELOPMENT OF METHODISM
IN THE OLD SOUTHWEST

1783-1824

CHAPTER I

METHODISM CROSSES THE ALLEGHENIES
1783-1799

The conversion of John Wesley on May 24, 1738, was the first event in a train of development which led to the establishment of the Methodist Church in England. The significance of this event for America is shown by the fact that 130 years after Wesley's conversion Ulysses Simpson Grant said that in the United States there were three political parties, the Republican, the Democratic, and the Methodist Church. From its English beginning, Methodism, held close in the heart of Irish and English immigrants,[1] established itself on the Atlantic Coast of North America, invaded the Western Valley, set up its institutions, and directed both the physical and spiritual life for millions of restless men. It was not, however, until after the close of the Revolution that the position of Methodism in America became secure.[2] The semblance of relations with the Church of England and the close connections between Wesley and his homeland[3] caused people to hesitate before aligning themselves with the newly formed Methodist societies, which were suspected by many of being friendly to the loyalist cause.[4] In spite, however, of the suspicion and prejudice from which it suffered, Methodism grew with the colonies, and at the close of the Revolution had eighty-three preachers and 14,988 members, an increase of 13,838 members in eleven years.[5]

---

1 See S. T. Duvall, *The Methodist Episcopal Church and Education up to 1869* (New York, 1928), 13.

2 For the demoralizing effect of the Revolution see W. L. Grissom, *History of Methodism in North Carolina* (Nashville, 1905), ch. iv; Jessie Lee, *A Short History of the Methodists in the United States of America: Beginning in 1766 and Continued Till 1809* (Boston, 1810), 62.

3 For Methodism in this period see P. G. Mode, *The Frontier Spirit in American Christianity* (New York, 1923), 383; L. W. Bacon, *A History of American Christianity* (New York, 1897), 199-202; Duvall, *The Methodist Church and Education*, 14-15; S. W. Coggeshall, "A Review of the Rise and Progress of American Methodism," *Methodist Magazine*, XX (1838), 269-271. See, also, C. H. Van Tyne, "Influence of the Clergy, and of Religious and Sectarian Forces, on the American Revolution," *American Historical Review*, XIX (1912-1913), 44-64.

4 For Wesley's attitude toward the Revolution see his "Calm Address to the American Colonies," *The Works of the Rev. John Wesley A. M., Sometime Fellow of Lincoln College, Oxford* (Third edition, 14 vols., London, 1831), XI, 80-80. Also, see J. M. Buckley, *History of Methodism* (2 vols., New York, 1898), I, 158-168.

5 *Minutes of the Annual Conferences of the Methodist Episcopal Church for the Years 1773-1828* (New York, 1840), 5, 20. This is volume I of the *Minutes*.

When Wesley found that he could not induce the bishops of the Established Church to ordain men for work in America, he changed his views and later (1785) declared, "I firmly believe I am a scriptural *episcopos,* as much as any man in England or Europe."[6] Thereupon, he "firmly fixed his eye, and proceeded to take measures for executing his resolution."[7] In order to send over ordained preachers "He deliberately assumed and exercised the power of ordination, contrary to the canons of the Church of England, of which he was a member and a minister."[8] Thomas Coke, a Doctor of Civil Law and a Presbyter of the Church of England, was ordained and sent to America as a superintendent with full power to ordain others and to administer the sacraments of baptism and of the Lord's Supper.[9] Coke together with Richard Whatcoat and Thomas Vasey, elders, reached New York on November 3, 1784. Eleven days later Coke, the only child of a wealthy house, and Asbury, the only son of an English gardener, met for the first time at Barratt's Chapel, near Frederica, Delaware.[10]

As soon as Wesley's plans for Methodism in America were made known to Asbury, a conference was called in Lovely Lane Chapel, Baltimore.[11] There on the motion of John Dickens it was voted unanimously to form the Methodist Episcopal Church in the United States of America. Asbury declined Wesley's appointment as a superintendent and also refused to submit to

---

[6] *Works of John Wesley,* XIII, 220; T. A. Kerley, *Conference Rights; or, Governing Principles* (Nashville, 1898), 63.
[7] See Samuel Drew, *Life of the Rev. Thomas Coke, D. D.* (New York, 1837), 63, for Wesley's point of view.
[8] J. J. Tigert, *A Constitutional History of American Episcopal Methodism* (Nashville, 1894), 161. Charles Wesley's opposition to his brother's action finds expression in a stanza:
"How easily bishops are made,
By man or woman's whim!
Wesley his hands on Coke hath laid
But who laid hands on him?"
Quoted in A. W. Nogler, *The Church in History* (Cincinnati, 1929), 190.
[9] See Drew, *Life of Thomas Coke,* 64, for manner in which Coke first received Wesley's unprecedented appointment. Also T. B. Neely, *Doctrinal Standards of Methodism* (Chicago, 1918), 147-149. For the certificate given by Wesley to Coke see E. S. Tipple, *Francis Asbury, the Prophet of the Long Road* (New York, 1916), 134-135. Wesley's directions for procedure were set forth in his letter brought by Coke to America and addressed "To Dr. Coke, Mr. Asbury and our brethren in North America," *Minutes,* I, 21-22.
[10] For a splendid contrast between Coke and Asbury see Tipple, *Francis Asbury,* 140-141. The report of an eye witness to Coke and Asbury's first sight of each other is in Tigert, *Constitutional History of Methodism,* 182. For Asbury's account see Francis Asbury, *Journal of Rev. Francis Asbury* (3 vols., New York, 1852), I, 484.
[11] Famous in history as the Christmas Conference.

ordination without the concurrence of the American preachers. Democracy had already made too much headway in America to submit to arbitrary appointments, and Asbury wisely demanded that "his new position should be based upon the consent of the preachers, and not alone upon the jurisdiction of Mr. Wesley."[12] He thus insured favor with the people among whom he was to spend the remainder of his life. When asked to vote on the issue, the conference unanimously chose the son of the gardener of Wednesbury as a Bishop of the Methodist Church in America.[13]

Tigert contended that Wesley "did not intend the separation of the American and English Methodists into two communions," nor did he "include in his scheme the assembling of the American itinerants to pass judgment upon his proposals or plans," nor did he intend to originate an American General Conference.[14] American Methodism revolted against being controlled by its British founder and insisted upon working out its own destiny. Asbury, when aware of Wesley's desire to establish "a perpetual worldwide union of Methodists," did not think it "practical expediency to obey Mr. Wesley at three thousand miles distance."[15] Thus, through the leadership of Francis Asbury, the several annual conferences "unanimously agreed that circumstances made it expedient for us to become a separate body under the denomination of the Methodist Episcopal Church."[16]

No longer was the American branch to be hindered by British connections, British interferences, and unordained American ministers. The church in America was henceforth free to create its own bishops, to ordain its clergymen, and to adopt disciplines suitable to America's changing needs. It was to be

---

[12] Tigert, *Constitutional History of Methodism*, 183. Contrast this attitude of Asbury with that of the first annual American conference in 1773. *Minutes*, I, 5.
[13] Tipple, *Francis Asbury*, 151; Tigert, *Constitutional History of Methodism*, 231-232. For a general discussion of the episcopacy, formation, election, and authority see J. F. Berry, "The Methodist Episcopacy," *Christian Advocate*, CI (1926), 1128-1131.
[14] Tigert, *Constitutional History of Methodism*, 187-188, 191. For a thorough discussion of an opposite point of view see Kerley, *Conference Rights*, ch. iv. George Bancroft, *History of the United States of America* (6 vols., New York, 1888), VI, 160, says: "No sooner had the people of the United States been recognized as a nation by the king of England himself, and the movement to found an American episcopacy had begun, than he [Wesley] burst the bonds that in England held him from schism, and resolved to get the start of the English hierarchy."
[15] Tigert, *Constitutional History of Methodism*, 232.
[16] *Minutes*, I, 21.

a democratic church, enjoying the freedom of a frontier workshop in which to labor.

The close of the American Revolution brought a new era to the West. The colonies were now faced with a new independence, and the necessity of developing some distinctive characteristics. The colonists found themselves best fitted to carry on the work of territorial expansion, and gradually they crept farther over the Allegheny barrier. Kentucky and Tennessee were admirably located to share in the westward extension, for the Cumberland Gap[17] was the chief outlet to the West, and through it the immigrants, straitened in finances, came seeking cheap but fertile lands. Here, chiefly in valleys watered and drained by the Tennessee, Cumberland, Kentucky, and Ohio rivers, was a future home for countless thousands; here, a democratic religion[18] would never fail to be a factor in the growth and well-being of its inhabitants.

The French and Indian War had scarcely closed (1763) before settlements were made beyond the mountains in what is now Kentucky and Tennessee.[19] William Bean built his cabin on the banks of the Little Watauga River in 1769. Daniel Boone had already hunted in Kentucky when Richard Henderson negotiated a private treaty with the Indians by which they ceded to him the greater part of present day Kentucky and a large section of Middle Tennessee.[20] Boone, the hunter, was followed by James Robertson, John Sevier, and William Blount, all land

---

17 Ellen Semple, *American History and Its Geographic Conditions* (New York, 1903), 65-69, *passim;* W. A. Pusey, *The Wilderness Road to Kentucky; Its Location and Features* (New York, 1921).

18 "Instituted in England by a narrow High-Church clergyman of the established church, its preachers were simply a company of lay missionaries under the command of John Wesley; its adherents were members of the Church of England . . . and its chapels and other property . . . were held under iron-bound title deeds, subject to the control of John Wesley and the close corporation of preachers . . . . It seems hardly worthy of the immense political sagacity of Wesley that he should have thought to transplant this system unchanged into the midst of circumstances so widely different as those which must surround it in America." Bacon, *History of American Christianity,* 217-218. Compare the foregoing with an account of the democratic religion upheld by Methodists in America by 1800 in Alfred Brunson, *A Western Pioneer: or, Incidents of the Life and Times of Rev. Alfred Brunson* (2 vols., New York, 1872-1879), I, 38-43.

19 The best account of the settlement of Kentucky and Tennessee is still the romantically written volumes of Theodore Roosevelt, *Winning of the West* (6 vols., New York, 1905). A good general account is F. L. Paxson, *History of the American Frontier,* 1763-1893 (Boston, 1924).

20 See Archibald Henderson, *Conquest of the Old Southwest* (New York, 1920). An extremely partial account due no doubt to the blood relation between Richard Henderson, the chief character in the conquest, and the author.

speculators.[21] So strong an aptitude did the Westerners show for self-government that they made several attempts for independence[22]—such as Watauga (1772), Transylvania (1775), and Franklin (1784)—without sanction from the states whose territory they had illegally acquired. Frontier grievances were remedied considerably when Kentucky was admitted into the Union in 1792[23] and Tennessee, in 1796.

The early settlers in Kentucky and Tennessee came chiefly from Virginia and North Carolina; hence, their ancestry was English. In other parts of the mountains "the Scotch-Irish element was ascendant; and this contentious, self-reliant, hardy backwoods stock, with its rude and vigorous forest life, gave the tone to Western thought in the Revolutionary era."[24] The impression has been made that many of these early settlers were convicts, but "it must be remembered that many of them were only convicted of having belonged to Cromwell's army, or of persisting in attending religious meetings conducted by dissenters."[25] Into this new country, however, the people went for the specific purpose of bettering their fortunes—and that, in most cases, meant stress on material rather than moral and spiritual life. And in this tide of settlers who swept through the Appalachian gateways were Methodist members, exhorters, and both local and itinerant preachers. Each year the frontier line moved westward, and every move was an additional challenge to the Methodist circuit rider to follow closely on the heels of the settlers.

While historians have generally agreed that the Presbyterians were the first to establish places of worship in Tennessee, the question of which denomination furnished the first minister is

---

21 Land speculation needs an enormous amount of study. Its importance can hardly be exaggerated. See A. P. Whitaker, *The Spanish American Frontier*: 1783-1795 (New York, 1927), 47-57 *et. seq.*; also his article, "The Muscle Shoals Speculation," *Mississippi Valley Historical Review*, XIII (1926-1927), 365-386; T. P. Abernethy, *From Frontier to Plantation in Tennessee* (Chapel Hill, 1932), *passim;* C. S. Driver, *John Sevier, Pioneer of the Old Southwest* (Chapel Hill, 1932), chs. iv, viii.
22 Two of the best monographs on this subject are those of F. J. Turner, "Western State Making in the Revolutionary Era," *Amer. Hist. Rev.*, I (1895-1896), 70-87, 251-269; and G. H. Alden, "The State of Franklin," *ibid.*, VIII (1902-1903), 271-289.
23 See Whitaker, *Spanish American Frontier*, 122.
24 Turner, "Western State Making in the Revolutionary Era," *Amer. Hist. Rev.*, I (1895-1896), 73.
25 W. G. Frost, "Our Contemporary Ancestors in the Southern Mountains," *Atlantic Monthly*, LXXXIII (1899), 315.

one of much debate. By 1780 the Presbyterians had sent into this new country Samuel Doak through whose efforts Doak's Academy,[26] the first literary institution in the Mississippi Valley, was established.[27]

The first Methodist effort in America which directly affected Tennessee was the annual conference of 1783, held first at Ellis' Preaching House in Sussex County, Virginia, and later at Baltimore.[28] This conference established the Holston Circuit embracing the settlements on the Watauga, Holston, and Nolichucky rivers, with a few appointments on the head-waters of the New River. Jeremiah Lambert was stationed on this far-flung circuit in Southwest Virginia and East Tennessee. Taking charge of his circuit with a membership of sixty, who had been previously gathered by unknown Methodist preachers, Lambert added only sixteen new communicants during his year's service. The facts of Lambert's life are obscure. He was admitted as a traveling preacher in Delaware in 1781; was received into full connection at the conference held at Ellis' Meeting House in 1782; and served his last charge in Antigua, an island in the West Indies.[29] His death in 1786 is noted in the *Minutes* by a short obituary.[30] In the year of Lambert's death his work in Tennessee was materially realized when Acuff's Chapel, the first Methodist church in Tennessee, was erected in Sullivan County, near the present Blountsville.[31]

In a group of Irish immigrants which had come to America in 1771, there had been a young man named Francis Asbury. Seventeen years later Asbury, in the office of bishop of the Methodist Episcopal Church, crossed the mountains to attend the first conference in the West, which was held at Keywood's or Cawood's on the Holston River in Washington County, Vir-

---

26 Later Washington College.
27 James Phelan, *History of Tennessee* (Boston, 1889), 218. See, also, W. A. Provine, "Tennessee's Earliest Educational Institutions," *Tennesee Historical Magazine*, 2nd. series, II (1932), 165-178.
28 *Minutes*, I, 17.
29 J. B. McFerrin, *History of Methodism in Tennessee* (3 vols., Nashville, 1871-1874), I, 28; R. N. Price, *Holston Methodism from its Origin to the Present Time* (5 vols., Nashville, 1912-1913), I, 94, 97-98; H. N. McTyeire, *A History of Methodism* (Nashville, 1884), 353.
30 *Minutes*, I, 25.
31 Oliver Taylor, *Historic Sullivan* (Bristol, Tennessee, 1909), 180; McFerrin, *Methodism in Tennessee*, I, 105.

ginia, on May 13-15. Concerning this Asbury wrote in his journal·

> The people are in disorder about the old and new State: two or three men, it is said, have been killed. Came to Half-Acres and Keywood's where we held conference three days, and I preached each day. The weather was cold; the room without fire, and otherwise uncomfortable. We nevertheless made out to keep our seats, until we had finished the essential parts of our business.[32]

It is evident that Bishop Asbury did not allow the civil disturbances in Tennessee to hinder him, but held the conference with the few preachers who were in Holston, together with those from Kentucky.[33] Ramsey paid the following tribute to the timely arrival of the bishop and the soothing effects of this early conference:

> This first Conference west of the mountain—the novelty of such an assemblage . . . its mission of benignity and peace—the calm dignity and unpretending simplicity of the Venerable Bishop, all conspired to soothe, quiet and harmonize the excited masses, and to convert partizans and factionists into brothers and friends.[34]

The Baptists were the pioneers in the early religious work in Kentucky. Some Baptist ministers had entered Kentucky long before the decade of 1780-1790. Among them was William Hickman who preached at Harrodsburg as early as 1776.[35] Seven years later Francis Clark, a Methodist local preacher, left Virginia and moved to Kentucky accompanied by his family and the families of several of his neighbors. Immediately upon settlement in Mercer County, Clark organized the first class in the far west and appointed John Durham as its leader.[36] In 1786 the Kentucky Circuit was organized with James Haw as presiding elder and Benjamin Ogden as circuit preacher.[37] At the close

---

32 Asbury, *Journal*, II, 32-33.
33 G. G. Smith, *Life and Labors of Francis Asbury* (Nashville, 1896), 110.
34 J. G. M. Ramsey, *The Annals of Tennessee* (Philadelphia, 1860), 417.
35 John Taylor, *A History of Ten Baptist Churches of Which the Author Has Been Alternately a Member* (Frankfort, Kentucky, 1823), 48; W. B. Allen, *A History of Kentucky Embracing Gleanings, Reminiscences, Antiquities, Natural Curiosities, Statistics, and Biographical Sketches* (Louisville, 1872), 176.
36 A. H. Redford, *The History of Methodism in Kentucky* (3 vols., Nashville, 1868-1870), I, 26; Z. F. Smith, *History of Kentucky* (Louisville, 1886), 409.
37 *Minutes*, I, 26; Redford, *Methodism in Kentucky*, I, 27.

of the first year, ninety members were reported from this circuit, and the first decade brought the enrollment to 1,707.[38]

The earliest Kentucky Conference met in the spring of 1790 at Masterson's Station, five miles from Lexington.[39] To attend this conference Asbury again crossed the mountains, the second of thirty-one times during his life.[40] The trip required a journey of eight days through a wilderness containing such savage Indians that a company of ten men was deemed necessary to guard the bishop from them. The markers of twenty-four graves observed on the route gave evidence of earlier travelers who had met with the ever-present danger.[41] The conference to which Asbury traveled was composed of six preachers—Francis Poythress, James Haw, Wilson Lee, Stephen Brooks, Barnabas McHenry, and Peter Massie.[42] The Bishop was highly pleased with his labors in Kentucky. At this meeting he fixed upon the plans for the future Bethel College, and obtained by subscription upward of three hundred pounds in land and money for its establishment.[43]

In spite of the fact that two preachers were assigned to Kentucky in 1785, Methodism did not reach West Tennessee (now known as, and called hereafter, Middle Tennessee) until 1787 when Benjamin Ogden came down from Kentucky to preach to the Cumberland settlements. His circuit embraced, besides Nashville, all the forts and settlements on the north side of the Cumberland River, as far as Clarksville on the west, and Gallatin on the east.[44] This territory now includes the counties of Sumner, Davidson, and Robertson. From 1786 to 1834 Ogden, "a plain strong effective preacher,"[45] could be heard beseeching men to join the banner of Christ.[46] The first Methodist church in

---
38 *Minutes*, I, 28, 74.
39 Redford, *Methodism in Kentucky*, I, 67.
40 Tipple, *Francis Asbury*, 187.
41 Asbury, *Journal*, II, 83.
42 Redford, *Methodism in Kentucky*, I, 68.
43 Asbury, *Journal*, II, 85.
44 John Wooldridge (ed.), *History of Nashville, Tennessee* (Nashville, 1890), 453; W. W. Clayton, *History of Davidson County, Tennessee* (Philadelphia, 1880), 324; J. M. Anderson, "The Heroes of the Ministry in the Early History of Tennessee Methodism," *Tennessee Conference Journal*, 1912, p. 110; Smith, *History of Kentucky*, 409.
45 A. W. Putnam, *History of Middle Tennessee* (Nashville, 1859), 282.
46 Ogden and Haw, the first Methodist traveling preachers to set foot on Kentucky soil became dissatisfied and withdrew with James O'Kelly. Haw ended his days as a Presbyterian preacher, while "Ogden back-slid, quit preaching, kept a groggery, and became wicked." Later during a revival he joined the church

Nashville was built in 1789 or 1790, a stone building that stood somewhere near the present square.[47]

The growth of Methodism was sufficiently general to touch all the Central Western states at about the same time. As early as 1796 a class of ten was formed in Ohio, near the town of Milford, by Francis McCormick, a local preacher, who had emigrated from Virginia to Kentucky and from there to Ohio.[48] Two years later Reverend John Kobler, presiding elder of the Kentucky District, laid the foundations for Methodism in that section by forming the Miami Circuit,[49] which included the cities of Dayton and Cincinnati.[50] Through the instrumentality of John Collins, a local preacher from New Jersey, who had settled on the East Fork of the Little Miami, several new preachers were enlisted[51] so that by 1807 an annual conference was held in Chillicothe, at which time the Ohio District had 3,884 members and seventeen preachers.[52] In early Ohio history this Methodist movement had a large part because Edward Tiffin, a local Methodist preacher, was chosen as the first governor of that state.[53]

The Methodist circuit riders went not only north from Kentucky and Tennessee into the Ohio Valley but also south into the Mississippi Territory. At the South Carolina Conference in January, 1797, Asbury selected Tobias Gibson for missionary work in the Southwest.[54] After traveling six hundred miles on

---

again, was licensed to preach, and died in Methodist harness. See Peter Cartwright, *Autobiography of Peter Cartwright the Backwoods Preacher* (ed. by W. P. Strickland, New York, 1857), 39-40; J. B. Finley, *Sketches of Western Methodism; Biographical, Historical and Miscellaneous* (ed. by W. P. Strickland, Cincinnati, 1857), 48; A. H. Redford, *Western Cavaliers; Embracing the History of the Methodist Episcopal Church in Kentucky from 1832-1844* (Nashville, 1876), 17, 24-25.

47 John Carr, *Early Times in Middle Tennessee* (Nashville, 1857), 66. Carr's book has considerable value, but is very inaccurate as it was written wholly from memory.

48 Nathan Bangs, *History of the Methodist Episcopal Church* (4 vols., New York, 1857), II, 77-78.

49 See Finley, *Sketches*, 103-104, for Kobler's visit to Ohio, and 163-177 for a sketch of the life of Kobler. Extracts from Kobler's *Journal* (in M. P. Gaddis, *Foot Prints of an Itinerant*, Cincinnati, 1874, pp. 504-511) give a highly interesting account of his Ohio trip. A brief history of the early development of Methodism in Ohio may be found in the *Methodist Magazine*, V (1822), 314-316, 350-353.

50 In 1790 the Presbyterians had organized a society in Cincinnati which met regularly every Sabbath. See Finley, *Sketches*, 102-103, 105. Finley devotes pages 102-128, 193-201 to the origin and progress of Methodism in Cincinnati.

51 Bangs, *History of the Methodist Church*, II, 79.

52 *Minutes*, I, 152, 159, 161.

53 See W. E. Gilmore, *Life of Edward Tiffin, First Governor of Ohio* (Chillicothe, 1897); Finley, *Sketches*, 260-287.

54 J. G. Jones, *A Complete History of Methodism as Connected with the Mississippi Conference of the Methodist Episcopal Church, South* (2 vols., Nashville, 1887). I, 24.

horse-back, Gibson reached the Cumberland settlements near Nashville. There he sold his horse; put his saddle and baggage into a canoe; and paddled himself down the Cumberland into the Ohio and from there into the Mississippi, where he was picked up by a boat and landed at Natchez seven hundred miles from his place of embarkation.[55] In the year of his arrival the vast circuit to which he had been sent reported sixty members.[56] There was not another Methodist minister—either local or itinerant—within five hundred miles, and for four years Gibson did not see a preacher of his faith.[57]

The turn of the century found Methodism in Tennessee and Kentucky organized into six circuits with a membership of approximately 2,500.[58] This great task was accomplished principally by the Methodist itinerant with his indefinite territory. The people either were too poor or were not inclined to support a stationed preacher; the church answered the situation by making out a circuit, putting a rider on it, and bidding him cover it at least once a month, preaching at every possible opportunity. This system secured the greatest religious expansion at the least expense and triumphed in competition with the Presbyterian and Baptist systems.

It has been said that the people of the frontier lived in a sort of religious Garden of Eden and resisted all temptation to feast now and then upon forbidden fruit. That they were not without their vices, however, is indicated by an extract from the *Journal* of Asbury, who on a trip through East Tennessee in 1797 wrote:

> I am of opinion it is as hard, or harder, for the people of the west to gain religion as any other. When I consider where they came from, where they are, and how they are, and how they are called to go farther, their living unsettled, with so many objects to take their attention, with the health and good air they enjoy; and when I reflect that not one in a hundred came here to get religion, but rather to get plenty of good land,

---

55 Bangs, *History of the Methodist Church*, II, 82; Jones, *Methodism in Mississippi*, I, 26-27; A. J. Pickett, *History of Alabama and Incidentally of Georgia and Mississippi from the Earliest Period* (Birmingham, 1900), 473.
56 *Minutes*, I, 95.
57 Jones, *Methodism in Mississippi*, I, 60, 66-67. Gibson died from exposure in April, 1804. See *Minutes*, I, 125-126, for a sketch of his life.
58 *Ibid.*, I, 97.

I think it will be well if some or many do not eventually lose their souls.[59]

This lack of interest in religion was realized by some of the great leaders of the day. A speech by Dr. Lyman Beecher in the United States Senate, on March 1, 1825, reflected the fear that the nation as a whole might suffer because of a failure of the West to direct aright its institutions. He pleaded for aid and for workers to be sent to these Western people in order that proper institutions might be formed, which, in turn, would influence the mind, conscience, and heart.[60]

Life on the frontier was hard and primitive. The typical house was the cabin built of round logs, the chinks of which were filled with mortar of clay. Not all of them were equipped with floors[61] and, even worse, many were not clean. An insight into their crowded, filthy and barely livable conditions is given by Asbury after he caught the itch on the way to the Western Conference in 1803. He wrote: "Considering the filthy houses and filthy beds I have met with in coming from the Kentucky Conference, it is perhaps strange that I have not caught it twenty times."[62] At the windows of the houses wooden shutters were used as there was no glass; later, paper smeared with bear's grease was used over the apertures.[63] Furniture was of the roughest sort; beds were made of slabs laid across poles; knives and forks were rare; and plates were wooden.[64] Frontier food was often extremely unpalatable. It was not any wonder that young Henry Bascom (later Bishop) wrote in his diary, "Tried to study, but too much confusion, tried to pray in the family but

---

59 Asbury, *Journal*, II, 342. See Jones, *Methodism in Mississippi*, I, 173, for different types of people in the early Mississippi Territory. For other regions see J. B. Finley, *Autobiography of Rev. James B. Finley, or, Pioneer Life in the West* (ed. by W. P. Strickland, Cincinnati, 1854), 196, 330; T. M. Eddy, "Influence of Methodism Upon the Civilization and Education of the West," *Methodist Review* (New York, 1857), XXXIX, 281-282. I have disregarded the various titles under which the *Methodist Review* was published in the South and North. In order to facilitate the reading I have regularly made reference to the *Methodist Review* (New York) or the *Methodist Review* (Nashville).
60 For a portion of Dr. Beecher's speech see F. J. Turner, *The Frontier in American History* (New York, 1921), 35.
61 Paxson, *The American Frontier*, 114.
62 Asbury, *Journal*, III, 132. For filth on the frontier see M. M. Henkle, *The Life of Henry Bidleman Bascom* (Nashville, 1860), 49.
63 A small boy who saw this for the first time ran home and cried aloud, "Granny, come see a house with 'specs on .'" Fannie Duncan, *When Kentucky Was Young* (Louisville, 1928), 109.
64 R. S. Cotterill, *History of Pioneer Kentucky* (Cincinnati, 1917), 246; W. H. Perrin, J. H. Battle, G. C. Kniffen, *History of Kentucky* (Louisville, 1886), 212.

felt too dull—tried to eat breakfast, but the victuals were too dirty for any decent man to eat."[65] The dress of these people was necessarily simple since their clothes were made of homespun cotton and linen.[66] Peter Cartwright stated that the Methodists "wore no jewelry, no ruffles" and so uncompromising was he concerning the demand of the *Discipline* for simplicity in dress that he forced a woman to alter her dress before she was permitted to attend a love feast.[67]

There was a dearth of books on the frontier; especially was this true of Bibles up to 1817, when the American Tract Society was organized in the East to aid Western people in securing religious literature.[68] An examination of the files of the *Knoxville Gazette* for 1791-1796[69] reveals the scarcity of book publicity, a fact which may indicate that there was little interest in books and their sale. The few advertisements printed display the usual household handbooks of spellers, arithmetics, and Bibles. To many a thrifty Tennessean such advertisements did not justify the expense, and, for economy's sake, frequently book lists were topped by blazers of whiskey and card bargains.

In the observance of the Sabbath the day was considered only as one "set apart for hunting, fishing, horse racing, cardplaying, balls, dances, and all kinds of jollity and mirth."[70] In some sections markets on Sunday were as common as those on week days.[71] "There was much loosening of the bonds, social, political, moral, religious."[72] The pioneer was brusque in manners, illiterate, untrained, and possessed by strong impulses. His religion was of the same nature and so featured as to fit in with the "storminess of its weather beaten professor."[73] The churches

---

65 Henkle, *Life of Bascom*, 58. Regarding this home Bascom continued in his diary: "The old man is an idiot, the old woman a scold, one son a drunkard, the other a sauce-box, and the daughter a mother without a husband."
66 James Hall, *Sketches of History, Life and Manners in the West* (2 vols., Philadelphia, 1835), I, 227.
67 Cartwright, *Autobiography*, 76. See a *Discipline* for any of the early years of Methodism (for example the one for 1812, pp. 96, 99-100) for regulations of jewelry and dress. Also, see "Tyranny of Fashion," *Holston Messenger*, III (1828), 73-74.
68 Edward Channing, *A History of the United States* (7 vols., New York, 1907-1932), V, 226; McTyeire, *History of Methodism*, 563.
69 These may be found in the library of the Tennessee Historical Society at Nashville.
70 Cartwright, *Autobiography*, 25.
71 Brunson, *Western Pioneer*, I, 273.
72 Roosevelt, *Winning of the West*, IV, 24.
73 W. M. Green, *Life and Papers of A. L. P. Green* (Nashville, 1887), 16.

were filled by people voluntarily supporting their chosen denominations. European and English travelers failed to see these people with the proper perspective, and as a result, the accounts that were sent back in several instances[74] failed to give credit for the better features of frontier society. On the other hand, there is the danger of claiming too much for the West. There are those people who fondly believe that America, and more especially the West, has always been the home of religious liberty, but "religious toleration has never been the dominant characteristic of the American people."[75] Always there have been preachers and teachers trying to prove the value of their religion and the uselessness of that professed and propounded by someone else. The constitution of the state of Franklin, written in 1785, held that no man who denied the existence of God might hold office in that state. The constitution of Tennessee of 1796 took a step decidedly forward in behalf of religious liberty when it declared that no religious test should be a qualification for any office. This political statute providing for religious tolerance might indicate either the presence of intolerance or a fear that it might arise.[76]

Into such social, political, and religious conditions Methodism threw the whole of its strength,[77] confident that these conditions could be met and conquered through the Methodist system of itineracy, which made it possible to reach far distant and scattered settlements. It was from the great class of non-church members that Methodism was to draw its greatest numbers.[78] Its appeal was reinforced by the practical good it accomplished. A fervid writer stated that: "It alone was so organized as to be able to follow step by step this movable population, and to carry the

---

[74] See such accounts as Isaac Weld, *Travels through the States of North America and the Provinces of Upper and Lower Canada During the Years* 1795, 1796, and 1797 (London, 1799); Thomas Hamilton, *Men and Manners in America* (London, 1843); and others. One of the best recent collections of travels in the West is S. C. Williams (ed.), *Early Travels in the Tennessee Country,* 1540-1800 (Johnson City, Tennessee, 1928).

[75] Richardson Wright, *Hawkers and Walkers in Early America* (Philadelphia, 1927), 144; V. L. Parrington, *The Colonial Mind,* 1620-1800 (New York, 1927), *passim.*

[76] Thomas Jefferson deplored the narrow religious views and laws regulating freedom of worship. See his *Notes on the State of Virginia* (Philadelphia, 1794), 231-232.

[77] See Abel Stevens, *Life and Times of Nathan Bangs, D. D.* (New York, 1863), 102.

[78] Methodism did not draw any large number of the upper or wealthy class until the second and third decades of the nineteenth century, due to a variety of causes such as education of its ministers, and its stand on slavery.

gospel even to the most distant cabin. It alone could be present whenever a grave was opened or an infant found in its cradle."[79]

As the population increased so did the circuits and preachers. The two preachers sent to serve Kentucky and Tennessee in 1786 were increased to thirteen within ten years.[80] In 1796 the two Tennessee circuits, Cumberland and Green, reported 505 white and forty-five colored members; while for the five Kentucky circuits—Kirkstone, Danville, Lexington, Limestone, and Salt River—the membership was composed of 1,666 whites and eighty-four colored, a grand total for the two states of 2,296.[81] This phenomenal increase was doomed to be halted, for as early as 1790 Methodism had met with the opposition of several sects.[82] Another obstacle was the defection in a prominent and influential preacher, James O'Kelly, a man of considerable ability, who objected to the appointing power of the bishops from which there was no recourse. He devised a plan by which a preacher who was dissatisfied with his appointment might appeal to the conference over the bishop's authority. When the General Conference of 1792 refused to adopt his plan, O'Kelly withdrew from the church, and formed a separate party called Republican Methodists. This reformation project attracted to its ranks some of the leading ministers and for a time actually threatened to disrupt the church.[83]

The first General Conference met in the fall of 1796[84] and to it the districts of Kentucky and Tennessee sent representatives to report their successes and failures, and to plead for more preachers. The next year Asbury pushed into Middle Tennessee and there found a spiritual dearth that gave rise to the passage expressing his fear that a number of westerners would lose their

---

79 Quoted by W. W. Sweet (*The Rise of Methodism in the West*, Cincinnati, 1920, p. 22) from "Peter Cartwright and Preaching in the West," *Meth. Rev.* (New York, 1872), LIV, 566-577 and LV (1873), 69-88.
80 *Minutes*, I, 70.
81 *Ibid.*, I, 69.
82 D. R. McAnally, *Life and Times of Rev. S. Patton and Annals of Holston Conference* (St. Louis, 1859), 164; Mode, *Frontier Spirit*, 118-119; Finley (*Sketches*, 54) gives an account of Burke's trouble with the Baptists around 1800.
83 James Porter, *The Revised Compendium of Methodism* (New York, 1875), 139-140; Anderson, "Heroes of Tennessee Methodism," *Tenn. Conf. Jour.*, 1912, p. 109; Cartwright, *Autobiography*, 32-33; Bangs, *History of the Methodist Church*, I, 351-356.
84 For this conference see *Journals of the General Conference of the Methodist Episcopal Church, 1796-1836* (New York, 1855), 11-29. This is the first volume of the conference journals.

souls. Throughout the western ranks there was a general decline in membership in proportion to population increase, and a recognized failure in spiritual efforts. Aid from sources ordinarily fruitful was not forthcoming; the newspapers printed no church notices and devoted little space to religious topics.[85] Besides those already mentioned there were many other reasons for this spiritual decline. The treaty of Greenville with the Indians in 1795 opened up a large section of the Northwestern Territory to colonization.[86] Into this region people from Tennessee and Kentucky immigrated in large numbers, thereby materially decreasing the church membership in the section from which they came. Furthermore, constant Indian wars had brought about a state of affairs that made for moral relaxation and neglect of worship. "Scenes of bloodshed and partizan animosity steel the heart against the commands of God."[87] The meager support given to the itinerants forced many of them when they married to settle and become part-time preachers. William Burke was the "first married preacher to travel with what the people and preachers called the incumbrances of a wife." He said, "Everything was thrown in my way to discourage me. The Presiding Elder thought I had better locate; for he said, 'The people would not support a married man.' "[88]

Between 1795 and 1800 the Church as a whole had gained only 4,603 members; at the same time the loss in preachers was twenty-six. Over this same four-year period Tennessee and Kentucky had suffered a loss of fifty-two members, while the number of preachers had dropped from fourteen to nine.[89] In 1800 the combined population of Tennessee and Kentucky was 326,557.[90] Of this number 2,307 white people and 177 colored

---

85 The *Knoxville Gazette* for 1791-1796 contains only two statements regarding church affairs. Compare these with the space devoted to the writings of Tom Paine. K. W. Dean (*Social and Economic Conditions in Kentucky as Reflected in the Newspapers*, 1788-1804, M. A. thesis, University of Chicago, 1925, pp. 28-29) found that of a total of five hundred issues of four Kentucky newspapers published between 1788-1804 none mentioned the great Kentucky revival. The scarcity of religious articles stands out in contrast to the murders, robberies, and runaway wives.
86 For disposition of the public lands see J. B. McMaster, *A History of the People of the United States* (7 vols., New York, 1885-1892), III, ch. xvi.
87 Ramsey, *Annals of Tennessee*, 730.
88 William Burke, *Autobiography* (Finley, *Sketches*), 53.
89 *Minutes*, I, 60, 61, 62, 92, 93, 94.
90 *Abstract of the Fourteenth Census of the United States* (Washington, 1923), 19.

persons were members of the Methodist Church.[91] Cotterill estimated that in Kentucky only one person out of three was a member of any church in 1792.[92] Rev. Daniel Rice, a Presbyterian clergyman in Kentucky from 1783 to 1816, lamented that he found few "reputable characters as Christians" or "who supported a credible profession of religion."[93] Certainly a dearth of religion had come over the "Great Western World."[94] A spiritual stimulant was needed, and this was found by 1800 in the Great Revival. The Methodists, Presbyterians, and Baptists lost themselves in the enormous process of soul winning on a huge scale.[95]

---

[91] *Minutes*, I, 93.
[92] Cotterill, *Pioneer Kentucky*, 243.
[93] R. H. Bishop, *An Outline History of the Church in the State of Kentucky* (Lexington, Kentucky, 1824), 68, 80.
[94] In 1800 in Kentucky, the statistics as compared with those of 1790 show a falling off of one hundred per cent in Baptist membership in proportion to the increase in population. See W. D. Nowlin, *Kentucky Baptist History*, 1770-1922 (Baptist Book Concern, 1922), 63.
[95] Catherine Cleveland, *The Great Revival in the West*, 1797-1805 (Chicago, 1916), is by far the best study of the Western religious upheaval in 1800.

CHAPTER II

THE PERIOD OF THE CAMP MEETING
1800-1811

The opening of Western lands and the consequent flow of migration over the Alleghenies demanded revisions and extensions in the government of the Methodist Church. One conference proved to be greatly inadequate; the territory was much too large for even the able bishop to cover well. In order to meet the demands of the new territory, the Western Conference was organized in 1800 and consisted of one district made up of thirteen circuits and eleven preachers who ministered to 2,930 members.[1] A remarkable growth reflected the urgent need for this new conference. A division was necessitated in twelve years after its formation,[2] for the single district had increased to ten, comprising seventy-one circuits, 101 preachers, and 30,741 members.[3] The territory of the Western Conference of 1800 was far-flung, including all of Kentucky west of the Kanawha, East and West Tennessee, the Natchez Missions in Mississippi, and all settled regions north and northwest of the Ohio. Fifteen hundred miles of hard riding would cover the district.

Because of manifold duties and the infirmities of age, Bishop Asbury had not been in the West since 1793, but he planned to attend the first meeting of the new conference which was to be held on October 4, 1800, at Bethel, Kentucky. Rumors of the James O'Kelly schism[4] continued to reach Asbury. The secession was gathering strength and attracting able men to its cause—one of whom was William McKendree, who had been in the ministry since 1788.[5] There is a belief that Asbury and the newly elected Bishop Whatcoat persuaded McKendree, then a presiding elder of a Virginia district, to go with them to the Western Conference in order to save him from the evils of

---

1 *Minutes,* I, 94, 97, 98.
2 For a map showing the Western Conference see Sweet, *Rise of Methodism,* 34.
3 *Minutes,* I, 211, 212.
4 Due to a fight against the powers of the bishops. See Robert Paine, *Life and Times of William McKendree* (Nashville, 1880), 131-132; Tigert, *Constitutional History of Methodism,* 258-263.
5 See E. E. Hoss, "Bishop William McKendree," *Meth. Rev.* (Nashville, 1915), LXIV, 40-74.

O'Kellyism, of which he had freely imbibed. McKendree made his advent into Western Methodism in this way. At the first conference McKendree was given supervision of the entire Western Conference, with the title of Presiding Elder of the Kentucky District. "Never was a more felicitous appointment made."[6] In 1808 he was elected bishop and served until his death in 1835.[7] The West was McKendree's special field of interest. There he labored and there he died.

After leaving Bethel on October 4, McKendree and Asbury entered Tennessee on October 16. Two days later Asbury preached at Parker's, where he was met by Brothers John McGee, Lugg, Jones, and Spier, local preachers, and together they had "a small shout in the camp of Israel." That week Asbury visited Nashville for the first time, and met there a congregation of "not less than one thousand people," who "were in and out of the stone church, which if it were floored, ceiled, and glazed would be a grand house." This welcome should have made Asbury's heart lighter, for he had been much discouraged on that trip and had written in his journal: "I have thought, as I rode along, that in travelling nearly six hundred miles, we had only six appointments; and at these but small congregations; have we wearied ourselves in vain?"[8]

The years following the war had been filled with readjustments accompanied by immorality, worldliness, and infidelity. For a long time the church had been able merely to hold its own. Separated from their Eastern homes, surrounded by uncleared lands and half-wild Indians, all of which required a spirit of unrelenting conquest, the early settlers had found no place along the mid-western frontier for any of the refinements of a more advanced social order.[9] Living had taken on the brittle meaning of mere existence. These sturdy pioneers had pushed into the new land to secure "elbow room"; but the new land not only supported man, it also required in return the absorption of his interest in material pursuits, leaving little opportunity for pursuits

---

6 Paine, *William McKendree*, 125-128, 135.
7 J. O. Andrews, "Bishop McKendree," *Meth. Rev.* (Nashville, 1859), XIII, 161-170.
8 Asbury, *Journal*, II, 475, 476.
9 J. F. Cook, *Old Kentucky* (New York, 1908), 137.

of spiritual interests.[10] Settlements were far apart; frequently a whole winter was passed without the sight of a new face. Routine became a torture and monotony an instrument of madness. Sunday was welcomed as a day free from labor, but was given over to rowdy entertainment.[11] Man's social nature cried out in hunger—but was not fed.

With the turn of the nineteenth century the camp meeting came into existence[12]—an institution which was destined to provide for several years the chief social interest in a barren existence.[13] The origin of this form and manner of worship is obscure, and perhaps will not be settled to universal satisfaction as long as the Baptist, Presbyterian, and Methodist churches continue. The other denominations, nevertheless, must concede to the Presbyterians the honor of inaugurating the camp meeting in Kentucky and Tennessee.

The leader of the revival movement in this section was a minister of Presbyterian faith, James McGready, who had emigrated from North Carolina to Tennessee, and from there to Kentucky. In the latter state, he served jointly three churches, Gasper River, Muddy River, and Red River. McGready's diligent effort to revive the spiritual temper of his people began to produce striking results. An actual movement of awakening was distinctly noticeable by the spring of 1799.[14]

---

10 B. B. Tyler, *A History of the Disciples of Christ* (New York, 1894), 8; F. R. Cossitt, *The Life and Times of Rev. Finis Ewing* (Louisville, 1853), 103; Robert Davidson, *History of the Presbyterian Church in the State of Kentucky* (New York, 1847), 63.

11 Richard Henderson, while at Boonesborough in 1775, characterized the settlers as "a set of scoundrels who scarcely believed in God or fear the devil if we were to judge from their looks, words and actions." G. W. Ranck, *Boonesborough* (Louisville, 1901), 177. See, also, M. Butler, *Manners and Habits of the Western Pioneer* (MS. in Durrett Collection), 20; Tyler, *Disciples of Christ*, 4-5.

12 Richard McNemar, *The Kentucky Revival* (Concinnati, 1807), 23; *Meth. Mag.*, IV (1821), 190-191; J. P. McLean, "The Kentucky Revival and Its Influence on the Miami Valley," *Ohio Archeological and Historical Society Publications*, XIII (1903), 244-247; Cleveland, *The Great Revival*, 53 ff. A graphic description of a camp meeting is quoted in T. W. Preston, *Historical Sketches of the Holston Valley* (Kingsport, Tennessee, 1926), 166-169, from the autobiography of a Mrs. Julia A. Tevis, *Sixty Years in a School Room*. In studying any type of religion one should read the valuable work of William James, *The Varieties of Religious Experience* (New York, 1922).

13 Mode, *The Frontier Spirit*, 54; Cleveland, *The Great Revival*, 120 ff.; Cossitt, *Finis Ewing*, 66. An English observer called the camp meeting a species of "holy fair." See C. C. Sellers, *Lorenzo Dow The Bearer of the Word* (New York, 1928), 21.

14 "Extract of a Letter from the Rev. James McGready, a Presbyterian Minister, in Logan County, Kentucky, to the Rev. Dr. Coke," *Meth. Mag.* (London), 1803, pp. 181-184.

In this same spring, two brothers, John and William McGee, made a trip from Sumner County (now Smith), Tennessee through the barrens to Ohio. As they passed through Kentucky, they decided to stop for sacrament at a meeting house on the Red River. Here they first met McGready and saw the results of his evangelistic efforts.[15] These brothers—William, a Presbyterian and John, a Methodist—were highly pleased with McGready's method, and became so sincerely and seriously concerned that they came in July, 1800, from their home in Tennessee to attend McGready's four-day meeting held on Gasper River.[16] The fame of this meeting was to spread afar. The large crowds in attendance, and the distance from which many had come, required that some provisions be made for their accommodation. A suggestion was made that they all camp on or near the meeting ground. The suggestion was adopted; thus, the "camp meeting" came into being.

On returning to Drake's Creek in Middle Tennessee, William McGee in his enthusiasm began a camp meeting which lasted five days. McGee was assisted in this venture by four other Presbyterian preachers—Hodge, Craighead, Adair, and Rankin. On the last day of the meeting, October 20, William McKendree and Bishops Whatcoat and Asbury, traveling from the first Western Conference of the Methodist Episcopal Church, stopped at Drake's Creek. When invited to participate in the services, all three accepted the invitation of the Presbyterians to preach. Over one thousand people were present on this day, Monday; while two thousand had attended on the previous day. Concerning this occasion, Asbury recorded in his *Journal*:

> Yesterday, and especially during the night were witnessed scenes of deep interest. In the intervals between preaching, the people refreshed themselves and horses, and returned upon the ground. The stand was in the open air, embosomed in a a wood of lofty beech trees. The ministers of God, Methodists and Presbyterians,[17] united their labours, and mingled with the

---

15 John McGee to T. L. Douglass, June 23, 1820, *Meth. Mag.*, IV (1821), 190-191; M. H. Moore, *Sketches of the Pioneers of Methodism in North Carolina and Virginia* (Nashville, 1884), 237-248.
16 "Extract of Letter from McGready to Coke," *Meth. Mag.* (London), 1803, pp. 181-184; Cleveland, *The Great Revival*, 68.
17 See S. G. Ayres, "Francis Asbury and His Presbyterian Friends," *Meth. Rev.* (Nashville, 1917), LXVI, 467-475.

THE CAMP MEETING

child-like simplicity of primitive times. Fires blazing here and there dispelled the darkness, and the shouts of the redeemed captives, and the cries of precious souls struggling into life, broke the silence of midnight.... I rejoice that God is visiting the sons of the Puritans, who are candid enough to acknowledge their obligations to the Methodists.[18]

This was Asbury's first contact with a Western camp meeting. The device was destined to be a form of evangelization which was hastily, but briefly, to revolutionize the spiritual temper of the West.

The itinerant preachers had nowhere met with the enthusiasm which welcomed the birth of the camp meeting. In truth, it was not the spirit of man which hungered, but his gregarious nature. So with the coming of autumn,[19] "Age snatched his crutch; youth forgot his pastime; . . . bold hunters, sober matrons and little children flocked to the common centre of attraction."[20] Homes were deserted, settlements were temporarily abandoned, and fields left unworked,[21] for the whole countryside had turned out to the "holy fair." A wagon trip of thirty or forty miles [22] was a small price to pay for the social and spiritual tonic of a "religious holiday." Not many miles, however, were traveled alone, for the settlements were pouring out their folk;[23] one group would soon catch up with another, and the two would proceed together.[24] As the camp ground was neared the whole woods seemed alive with travelers, they passed and repassed on the road, and called to each other from great distances.[25] For

---
[18] Asbury, *Journal,* II, 476-477.
[19] Camp meetings usually began about the first of August.
[20] Davidson, *The Presbyterian Church in Kentucky,* 136.
[21] R. L. Rusk, *The Literature of the Middle Western Frontier* (2 vols., New York, 1925), I, 47; Theophilus Armenius (Thomas Hinde), "Account of the Rise and Progress of the Work of God in the Western Country," *Meth. Mag.,* II (1819), 223.
[22] R. B. McAfee, *The Life and Times of Robert B. McAfee and his Family Connections* (MS. in Durrett Collection), 277; Davidson, *The Presbyterian Church in Kentucky,* 134; John Brooks, *The Life and Times of the Rev. John Brooks Written by Himself* (Nashville, 1848), 39.
[23] P. G. Mode, "Revivalism as a Phase of Frontier Life," *Journal of Religion,* I (1921), 349-350; Finley, *Autobiography,* 363; B. W. Stone, *The Biography of Eld. Barton Warren Stone, Written by Himself with Additions and Reflections by Elder John Rogers* (Cincinnati, 1847), 37; T. S. Hinde, "Recollections of Mrs. Mary Todd Hinde," *Meth. Mag.,* XIII (1831), 128-131.
[24] *Meth. Mag.,* II (1819), 223; Davidson, *The Presbyterian Church in Kentucky,* 134-136.
[25] Rusk, *Literature of the Frontier,* I, 47-48; Davidson, *The Presbyterian Church in Kentucky,* 36; *Meth. Mag.,* II (1819), 223. Curiosity was no little factor in attracting the huge crowds. See Bangs, *History of the Methodist Church,* II, 107.

the late arrivals the road to the clearing was marked by blazing pine knots.[26] By evening the camp was in order, the wagons had been drawn up on the outer rim[27] and around each busied the women, gossiping with one another as they went about arranging the provisions and sleeping quarters.

If it were possible to pass in rapid succession from one camp meeting to another, the bold and salient features of each would form a composite picture similar to the one which follows.

Usually the politicians arrived early in the morning. Political rallies were unheard of, yet the politicians made much of the camp meeting with its large attendance.[28] Minds warmed with social contacts proved a fertile field for suggestion. Large crowds[29] furnished opportunities too rare to miss. Men who were usually non-committal and sparse of words suddenly grew loquacious; emotion long dormant sprang into life, and human contact seemed good. Late in the day the preacher reached the appointed meeting place; frequently he was worn out from his long ride and inadequate accommodations *en route*.[30] Facing dangers such as the average frontiersman did not encounter,[31] the circuit rider as a rule was as hale and hardy as the folk who gathered so eagerly about him.[32] Doubtless the night before had been spent in a cabin, infested with bed bugs, fleas and itchy children,[33] yet, he was fresh for his work, strong in purpose and tireless in effort.

Day and night were given over to the exercises of the revival. Besides three definite services in a day many prayer meetings were called;[34] and, if the spirit ran unusually high, the night

---

26 Sellers, *Lorenzo Dow*, 133.
27 McNemar, *Kentucky Revival*, 31.
28 Rusk, *Literature of the Frontier*, I, 47.
29 Twenty-five thousand attended the Cane Ridge, Kentucky, Camp Meeting in August, 1801. See J. R. Rogers, *The Cane Ridge Meeting House to which is Appended the Autobiography of B. W. Stone and a Sketch of David Purviance by William Rogers* (Cincinnati, 1910), 157; Finley, *Sketches*, 79.
30 W. W. Bennett, "Pioneer Methodism in Virginia," *Meth. Rev.* (Nashville, 1888), V, 90-91, 98; Eddy, "Influence of Methodism Upon the Civilization and Education of the West," *Meth. Rev.* (New York, 1857), XXXIX, 284; Sellers, *Lorenzo Dow*, 19-20.
31 W. H. Milburn, *Ten Years of Preacher-Life* (New York, 1859), 38-41; Finley, *Sketches*, 17-21.
32 J. F. Jameson, "The American Acta Sanctorum," *Amer. Hist. Rev.*, XIII (1907-1908), 294.
33 Asbury, *Journal*, III, 204.
34 Brooks, *Life and Times*, 40.

services continued until dawn.[35] Often old men, who knew that they could not last the night without occasional naps, brought their great coats, and wrapped in them lay down on the ground among the children.[36] Little preparation was made for the meals. The food was coarse, consisting principally of cornbread and jerked meat without salt[37]—a diet which alone would make for physical exhaustion and mental weakness. Under such strain, excited nerves could not be dulled but demanded additional stimuli. Sleepless nights and jaded appetites[38] played havoc with constitutions. Mental control gave way, and in its place reigned instability and suggestibility to a high degree.[39]

The night scenes were ones of color and tone.[40] Flickering camp fires and burning pine knots, which revealed wagons and tents, accentuated the density and darkness of the surrounding forest; voices sounded empty across the clearing; night closed in to engulf the circle of campers.[41] Men felt keenly a complete abandonment; a sense of dependence was overwhelming, and unconsciously they grew closer together.[42] Strength came from contact, familiarity sprang up everywhere, hundreds who had never seen each other's face before experienced a strange kinship.[43] The soil was fertile and the preachers worked with a more concentrated purpose.

"The very looks of a Methodist preacher would strike terror to the sinner's heart."[44] He was a veritable "son of Thunder" with hard eyes and a grave and unrelenting expression.[45] Dressed in a straight double breasted coat, short breeches and long stockings, his complete appearance was prepossessing and his whole

---

35 William Speer, *The Great Revival of* 1800 (Philadelphia, 1872), 43-44; Cleveland, *The Great Revival*, 53. A camp meeting in Georgia in 1807 continued through the whole of four nights. U. B. Phillips, *Plantation and Frontier* (Phillips and J. R. Commons, eds., *A Documentary History of American Industrial Society*, 10 vols., Cleveland, 1910), II, 284-286.
36 John Lyle, *Diary of Rev. John Lyle*, 1801-1803 (MS. in Durrett Collection), 57; Davidson, *The Presbyterian Church in Kentucky*, 159.
37 Cossitt, *Finis Ewing*, 69.
38 Lyle, *Diary*, 8, 10, 35, 54; McNemar, *The Kentucky Revival*, 25-26.
39 Cleveland, *The Great Revival*, 27-28, 118, 120 ff.; F. M. Davenport, *Primitive Traits in Religious Revivals* (New York, 1905), 64, 216, 222.
40 For McMaster's classic description of the camp meeting at night see his *History of the United States*, II, 578.
41 Hinde, "Recollections of Mrs. Mary Todd Hinde," *Meth. Mag.*, XIII (1831), 131; Bangs, *History of the Methodist Church*, II, 103.
42 Mode, *The Frontier Spirit*, 54.
43 McNemar, *The Kentucky Revival*, 31.
44 See a letter from John Carr in Brooks, *Life and Times*, 122.
45 Stone, *Biography Written by Himself*, 5; Brooks, *Life and Times*, 9-10.

attire suggested rigidity. From under his broad brimmed hat hung long locks of hair which reached to the shoulders.[46] Indeed his very presence checked levity, and from his entrance to the altar the congregation sat expectantly. The people considered him as being imbued with all knowledge of both Heaven and Hell—especially of the latter.[47] He usually spoke in a voice that rolled "like successive peals of grand thunder."[48] He harangued the people, hurling at them warning of the judgment; he accused, convicted, and consigned them to the hottest hells. The audience leaned forward appreciatively. He related his trials, experiences, travels, persecutions, sorrows, and joys.[49] Deep "Amens!" sanctioned the recital. Sanction grew to "Tell it Brother!" "Yes, I know it!" "Praise God!" "Come to the Lord!"[50]—the meeting was gathering momentum.[51] A demoniacal laugh, cold and piercing and devoid of mirth, coming from the right[52] where sat the women, would mean that the "holy laugh" had found expression.[53] With such applause the preacher waxed more eloquent; his voice, "as loud as any priest of Baal," rose to tumultuous volume, then dropped to a hissing whisper to run the range again. The crowd swayed to the rhythm of his voice; some rose to their feet to continue the tempo in a loose dance.[54] He plucked every emotion, yet he did not dare trust his oratory alone to convict sinners. To insure a successful beginning he had employed helpers upon whom he could depend to "Get up the 'rousements and bring the battle to the gate." With his zeal he electrified his

---

[46] W. M. Gewehr, "Some Factors in the Expansion of Frontier Methodism, 1800-1811," *Journal of Religion*, VIII (1928), 103; W. W. Sweet, *Circuit Rider Days in Indiana* (Indianapolis, 1916), 7, 34; Sellers, *Lorenzo Dow*, 17.
[47] D. H. Moore, "The Philosophy of Methodist Success," *Tenn. Conf. Jour.*, 1912, p. 170. For a description of the preaching of Lorenzo Dow see Jacob Young, *Autobiography of a Pioneer; or the Nativity, Experience, Travels, and Ministerial Labors of Rev. Jacob Young* (Cincinnati, 1857), 235-240; Mode, *The Frontier Spirit*, 54.
[48] Finley, *Autobiography*, 323.
[49] Timothy Flint, *Recollections of the Last Ten Years Passed in Occasional Residences and Journeyings in the Valley of the Mississippi* (Boston, 1826), 145.
[50] Sellers, *Lorenzo Dow*, 19; *Meth. Mag.*, II (1819), 223.
[51] E. A. Ross, *Social Psychology* (New York, 1914), 54-56.
[52] For division of the ground between the sexes see D. Sullins, *Recollections of an Old Man* (Bristol, Tennessee, 1910), 34; Peter Cartwright, *Fifty Years As a Presiding Elder* (New York, 1871), 235; Taylor, *Historic Sullivan*, 179.
[53] Stone, *Biography Written by Himself*, 41; S. R. Beggs, *Pages from the Early History of the West and Northwest* (Cincinnati, 1868), 36; Lyle, *Diary*, 65-66. See "Commencement of the Great Revival of Religion in Kentucky and Tennessee, in 1799," (a letter from John McGee to T. L. Douglass, June 23, 1820), *Meth. Mag.*, IV (1821), 189-191.
[54] Stone, *Biography Written by Himself*, 74.

congregation for three or four hours,[55] and in face of such onslaughts it wept and groaned, crying aloud for God's mercy, no doubt as much from terror of the loud voice and wild gesticulations as from its own conviction of sin.[56] A song was started, the parts were picked up, and the "Zion Traveller"[57] was in full spiritual swing. To suit the needs of the meeting new songs, in which the terrors of Hell were dwelt upon with almost brutal insistence, were improvised. The device had "struck fire," the crowd had been moved bodily.

At first sight these meetings presented to a spectator nothing but a scene of confusion.[58] It was impossible to handle the crowd, a "confused and careless audience,"[59] who talked and walked from place to place during the services. At times there were as many as six hymns being sung at once,[60] a dozen or more people praying aloud, "calling on the Lord" as it was termed, all of which was saturated with hysterical sobbing, convulsive groans, shrieks and screams that burst forth on all sides.[61] In such a din of intermingled exercises a loud voice could be heard only a few inches.[62] In order to reach the crowd several preachers were necessary.[63] Recruits were made from the laity.[64] Trees, stumps, and wagon beds served as pulpits in an emergency, and each new preacher had a gathering around him. As a man or woman began to shout the people turned to encourage the sufferer. With conversion sinners took the stand, or were hoisted to the shoulders of comrades and carried through the crowd while they declared the goodness of God.[65] Power to exhort was given to children. A little boy of twelve years with

---

55 Ramsey, *Annals of Tennessee*, 730.
56 Flint, *Recollections*, 145.
57 For this song see *Meth. Mag.*, XI (1828), 189. Wesley's interesting "Rules for Congregational Singing" may be found in *Meth. Mag.*, VII (1824), 189-190. For camp meeting songs see B. St. James Fry, "The Early Camp Meeting Song Writers," *Meth. Rev.* (New York, 1859), XLI, 401-413.
58 McNemar, *The Kentucky Revival*, 23; Lyle, *Diary*, 34, 42, 57, 65.
59 *Ibid.*, 22; *Meth. Mag.*, II (1819), 273.
60 Lyle, *Diary*, 30, 31, 40.
61 Finley, *Autobiography*, 303; *Impartial Review*, Nov. 29, 1806; McNemar, *The Kentucky Revival*, 31; Cartwright, *Autobiography*, 31.
62 Lyle, *Diary*, 61-65.
63 *Meth. Mag.* (London), 1803, p. 88; *Meth. Mag.*, II (1819), 273; Bangs, *History of the Methodist Church*, II, 108; Mode, *The Frontier Spirit*, 54; Stone, *Biography Written by Himself*, 37.
64 *Meth. Mag.*, II (1819), 273; E. G. Cutshall, *The Doctrinal Training of the Traveling Ministry of the Methodist Episcopal Church of the United States* (Ph. D. thesis, University of Chicago, 1922), 328.
65 Lyle, *Diary*, 64.

tears streaming from his eyes spoke until exhausted. With his last strength he cried out as he let fall a soggy handkerchief from his hand, "Thus, Oh Sinner shall you drop into hell, unless you forsake your sins and turn to the Lord."[66] Two small girls of nine and ten prayed and cried for mercy. After one had received relief from her sorrow, she turned to the other child and cried, "O, You Little Sinner, come to Christ."[67] A boy of seven was strangely affected, he spoke "a rapturous language" and dropped off into something like a hypnotic state from which he emerged into a religious ecstasy.[68] So well were children acquainted with the revival that even a child four years old "could give a more satisfactory account of the work than some grown people could."[69]

Before such manifestations sinners could not stand, nor could saints unflinchingly witness the miracles. Many bodily agitations accompanied the emotional excitement. The arms and legs stiffened, the pulse grew tremulous, and with a piercing scream the person fell to the ground, lying for many hours as if dead,[70] finally emerging with a shout, "I am saved!" The subject had undergone the "falling exercise," and by his collapse enjoyed the distinction of having passed through a spiritual transformation.[71] Several instances of striking phenomena helped create the reception for the camp meeting. A leader of a group of rowdies determined to break up a praying circle, so, mounting his horse, he rode swiftly into its midst. Cursing, he wheeled his horse in order to scatter the crowd better, but in a flash fell from his mount "as if smitten by lightning" and lay on the ground with "limbs rigid, his wrists pulseless, and his breath gone."[72] A woman became so curiously affected that she lay insensible for thirty-two hours. Fear was entertained by many that she would never recover; nevertheless, she came from the trance with the ease of a child waking from sleep, sprang to her feet and com-

---

[66] *Meth. Mag.*, II (1819), 224; McNemar, *The Kentucky Revival*, 25-26.
[67] *Ibid.*, 21.
[68] *Meth. Mag.* (London), 1803, pp. 125-126.
[69] *Ibid.*, 1798, p. 335.
[70] *Ibid.*, 1803, pp. 84-85; McNemar, *The Kentucky Revival*, 20. Falling exercises most common of all except shouting. See Cleveland, *The Great Revival*, 88.
[71] Finley, *Autobiography*, 303.
[72] He was apparently dead for thirty hours. See Finley, *Autobiography*, 364-365.

THE CAMP MEETING 27

menced shouting and singing.[73]

The falling spread as a contagion.[74] Men were struck down "like corn before a storm of wind."[75] The number that fell at Cabin Creek was placed at three thousand.[76] There was no escape from this gesture of the power. Many who through curiosity gathered around those fallen could not withstand the exhibition, and they became similarly affected. Some realized their weakness and susceptibility and sought to run away, but were overtaken in the woods.[77] With the number who "fell" increasing at each service (and it was admitted that these agitations became habitual),[78] the prostrate bodies were carried out and laid in rows[79] to prevent them from being trampled by the restless multitude. Portions of the ground were always spread with clean straw for the comfort of the mourners and those who were sure to fall.[80] This affectation led a preacher who participated in the camp meetings to fear that the bodily agitations would become at length the sport of lesser passions.[81]

Complete abandonment was given to the wildest enthusiasms.[82] Young people experienced a nervous reflex, an involuntary movement which was first noticed in the jerking of the forearm. They had felt the first touch of the "jerks," which was soon to grow to the disastrous extent of affecting every muscle in the body.[83] The victims were unable "to move from one place but jerked backward and forward in quick succession, their heads nearly touching the floor behind and before." If the head alone were affected, it jerked so quickly that "the features of the face could not be distinguished."[84] With such

---

73 *Ibid.*, 231.
74 Cartwright, *Autobiography*, 31; McNemar, *The Kentucky Revival*, 31; Cleveland, *The Great Revival*, 81.
75 *Meth. Mag.*, III (1820), 191; see, also, Bangs, *History of the Methodist Church*, II, 104.
76 *Meth. Mag.*, II (1819), 272.
77 Stone, *Biography Written by Himself*, 36-37; Bangs, *History of the Methodist Church*, II, 108; *Meth. Mag.* (London), 1803, pp. 85, 86.
78 Lyle, *Diary*, 26.
79 McNemar, *The Kentucky Revival*, 24; Bangs, *History of the Methodist Church*, II, 108; *Meth. Mag.* (London), 1803, p. 86.
80 *Meth. Mag.*, IV (1821), 192; Brooks, *Life and Times*, 26.
81 Lyle, *Diary*, 26.
82 Davidson, *The Presbyterian Church in Kentucky*, 159.
83 Brooks, *Life and Times*, 27-28; J. W. Monette, *History of the Discovery and Settlement of the Valley of the Mississippi* (2 vols., New York, 1848), II, 29; *Meth. Mag.* (London), 1803, p. 84.
84 Stone, *Biography Written by Himself*, 40.

distractions it is not surprising that once a neck snapped in the upheaval.[85] Neither men nor women, saints nor sinners were allowed to escape untouched. Wicked men, who smiled mockingly, were suddenly seized and in their cursing jerked "as though they'd be torn to atoms."[86] Perhaps this excitement was more prevalent among the women,[87] some of whom were so strong and violent in the exercise as to cause their dishevelled hair "to lash and crack like a whip, perfectly audible at a distance of twenty feet."[88] These spasmodic convulsions spread like wild fire. At one meeting twenty thousand people were reported to have "tossed to and fro like tumultuous waves of a sea in a storm."[89] Even the dogs which slunk around in the noisy crowd were not immune.[90] In wide areas near the camp ground, saplings were cut off breast high and used for support by the jerkers, who "kicked up the earth as a horse stamping flies."[91] The revolting exercises and practices became general, and the camp meeting scene increased to a degree of grossness. It is not surprising that intellectual people held themselves aloof.[92]

There can be no doubt that the attitude of the preacher had much to do with the presence of these nervous exercises. He was lamentably ignorant, but one step removed from illiteracy,[93] and his frantic zeal to convert far exceeded his devout prudence.[94] In his conduct there was little dignity;[95] he jerked,

---

[85] Cartwright, *Autobiography*, 50-51.
[86] Brooks, *Life and Times*, 27.
[87] Emotion of fear was forced to seek outlet, hence the exercises. See Davenport, *Primitive Traits*, 222.
[88] Monette, *The Valley of the Mississippi*, II, 29. See, also, Bennett, "Pioneer Methodism in Virginia," *Meth. Rev.* (Nashville, 1883), V, 97.
[89] Finley, *Autobiography*, 304.
[90] Beggs, *Pages from Early History*, 17.
[91] Lorenzo Dow, *History of Cosmopolite; or the Writings of Rev. Lorenzo Dow* (Cincinnati, 1858), 184. Cartwright (*Autobiography*, 48) recorded seeing five hundred persons jerking at one time. For use of saplings in the barking exercises see Stone, *Biography Written by Himself*, 41.
[92] Cleveland, *The Great Revival*, 27-28.
[93] Daniel Drake, *Pioneer Life in Kentucky. A Series of Reminiscential Letters from Daniel Drake . . . to His Children* (Cincinnati, 1870), 195; James Flint, *Letters from America Containing Observations on the Climate and Agriculture of the Western States* (R. G. Thwaites, *Early Western Travels*, IX, Cleveland, 1904), 196, 263, 264; Taylor, *Ten Baptist Churches*, 180; Rusk, *Literature of the Frontier*, I, 49; F. J. Turner, *The Rise of the New West* (New York, 1906), 109; J. A. Smith, *A History of the Baptists in the Western States East of the Mississippi* (Philadelphia, 1896), 76-77.
[94] *Impartial Review*, Nov. 29, 1806.
[95] At least momentary results were secured and lasting impressions made by men of no greater intellect than Lorenzo Dow, noted for his "outlandish exterior, his orang-outang feature, the beard that swept his aged breast," and "the piping treble voice, in which he was wont to preach what he called the kingdom." Quoted by Rusk, *Literature of the Frontier*, I, 49, from the *Western Monthly Magazine*, II, 223.

THE CAMP MEETING 29

danced, sang, and ran the whole gamut of the religious orgies. As an oracle he stood commanding and suggesting the frenzied action of his congregation. In him was a taint of vulgar popularity, and a willingness to cater to the depraved religious appetites. If salvation was expected to descend in a remarkable manner,[96] then he saw that the crowd got what it wanted.[97] He realized that the report of the success of the camp meeting was based on the number that "fell"; consequently, his chief interest lay in how many were caught in the "gospel net," and not how well they were caught. A large portion of the conversions was by no means permanent.[98] Some scarcely lasted the meeting; they "fell" one night only to be drunk two days later. After a lapse of a year it was difficult to find a good report of more than two or three professors of a certain camp meeting. Even 'Becca Bell "who often fell is now big with child to a wicked trifling schoolmaster of the name of Brown who says he'll be damned to hell if he ever marries her." To continue the narrative of some of the converts—"Raglin's daughter seems careless . . . Kitty Cummings got careless . . . Polly Moffitt was with child to Petty and died miserably in child bed."[99]

While the religious exercises were in progress within the encampment all manner of wickedness was going on without.[100] The large crowds contained many undesirables[101]—criminals, prostitutes, scapegallows[102]—the usual dregs of society that sift into a new country. There were many who had not been instructed in morals, and under the peculiar excitement, "the primitive surroundings fanned into flame primitive traits."[103] Under the cover of night the rowdies began their mischief.[104] A little group gathered just outside the clearing and threw hot fire brands into the meeting.[105] Others armed themselves and as a mob sauntered through the camp ground daring anyone to stop them.

---

96 See extract of a letter from Rev. James McGready, *Meth. Mag.* (London), 1803, pp. 181-184.
97 Sellers, *Lorenzo Dow*, 15-16.
98 Roosevelt, *Winning of the West*, VI, 175.
99 Lyle, *Diary*, 2, 40, 47-48.
100 Brooks, *Life and Times*, 42, 49.
101 Cossitt, *Finis Ewing*, 66.
102 Jones, *Methodism in Mississippi*, I, 173; Cleveland, *The Great Revival*, 30; Davidson, *The Presbyterian Church in Kentucky*, 160; Lyle, *Diary*, 24.
103 Davenport, *Primitive Traits*, 64.
104 Brooks, *Life and Times*, 41-42.
105 Lyle, *Diary*, 40.

Some turned vandals; and morning revealed horses with tails and manes clipped; bridles and saddles cut; and wagons taken apart.[106] Whiskey was brought to the grounds in barrels, hid out in the bushes and from there retailed to the multitude.[107] One thrifty Baptist came with his wagon loaded with liquor and "sold it out," whereupon, "many got groggy."[108] With their wild adventurous spirits additionally warmed, the unrulies became less restrained. At one meeting, after the conclusion of the night services, they entered the camping ground, and one climbed to the pulpit while others went into the altar and here responded with mocking "amens" to the imitative sermon. The church was soon faced with the task of protecting itself from such behavior.[109] In order to receive the protection of the state from the many bad men the benediction was never said until the close of the last service of the meeting, for as long as it was a worshipping assembly the state was its protector.[110] Trouble continued, however, until it became a part of every meeting to have a guard of respectable men, the use of which continued as late as 1820. It became dangerous for preachers to walk outside the camp alone, for there were some who were waiting to tell a slanderous tale.[111]

There was much evidence within the camp ground of the mingling of human passions that were "not sanctified by grace."[112] The high degree of moral laxity is revealed and the extent of misconduct is suggested in a plan made for "regulating the camp at night to prevent adulterous proceedings among the wicked.... When the people should sleep in the meeting house, divide the sexes and let the elders lie between but sit up at turns. At the camp around the stand, let the elders walk by turns as night watchers." The glow from the burning pine knots stuck in the hats of the watchmen revealed much to condemn. Under one altar were found six men lying with a strumpet. A man and

---
106 Brooks, *Life and Times*, 27, 41-42.
107 Lyle, *Diary*, 24; McNemar, *The Kentucky Revival*, 34; Brooks, *Life and Times*, 42. See, also, Horace Jewell, *History of Methodism in Arkansas* (Little Rock, 1892), 75.
108 Lyle, *Diary*, 24.
109 Brooks, *Life and Times*, 42, 138.
110 Sullins, *Recollections*, 37.
111 Brooks, *Life and Times*, 42, 57, 138-139.
112 Bangs, *History of the Methodist Church*, II, 13. The exercises in Kentucky ran into such wild excesses in some instances as to bring them into disrepute in the estimation of the more sober part of the community. Bangs, II, 159-160.

THE CAMP MEETING

a woman were discovered in a cornfield in the act of adultery. No doubt the vigilance committee was zealous in its tasks and unswerving in its pursuits. Perhaps a trace of pique touched Abram Hawks and Crass Wright when, after hastening for a candle, they discovered not a lewd couple but two men who had lain down to sleep.[113] Every where there was a loose interpretation of the seventh commandment.[114] It is generally believed by students of frontier history that illegitimate births took a sharp rise[115] after the camp meetings.

There were numerous occasions when Asbury had grave doubts of the value of the camp meeting. He warned audiences that feelings would not supply the neglect of family and closet worship. But when he witnessed the vast multitude with whom the church had made contacts, his doubts were overwhelmed, and rejoicing he wrote: "Bohemia has a great work—camp meetings have done this, glory to the Great I Am."[116]

Largely through the means of the camp meeting the membership of the Western Conference was increased approximately three-fold between 1801 and 1803. The average increase of two thousand a year necessitated a rapid division in territory. By 1803 four districts had been organized—Holston, Cumberland, Kentucky, and Ohio—consisting of twenty-six circuits.[117]

The results of the camp meetings had been so gratifying in the regions of Kentucky and Tennessee that further plans were laid for evangelical work in new sections. Two missionaries were sent to Natchez and one to Illinois by the Western Conference of 1803.[118] Benjamin Young was appointed as "Mitionary to the Illinoies," after being reprimanded with a "plaine talk for having said that he composed a certain song, when in truth he did not; that he had the misfortune to get his horses thye broke,

---

113 Lyle, *Diary*, 22, 23-24, 40.
114 Wright, *Hawkers and Walkers*, 155; Gilbert Seldes, *The Stammering Century* (New York, 1928), 49.
115 I have been unable to sustain this contention by published proof. For striking instances of excesses not given in this study see Finley, *Autobiography*, 236, 252, 257, 267, 291, 327; Rusk, *Literature of the Frontier*, I, 137-142; Redford, *Methodism in Kentucky*, II, 188; Flint, *Letters from America*, 263-264; Cartwright, *Autobiography*, 49-51, 77-78; Drake, *Pioneer Kentucky*, 195.
116 Asbury, *Journal*, III, 294.
117 *Minutes*, I, 103, 117, 119.
118 Asbury, *Journal*, III, 131.

when it was not so."[119] Tobias Gibson, who had volunteered in 1799 to go into the Mississippi Territory, worked there as the only itinerant preacher in that vast region until Moses Floyd was sent to his aid in 1803.[120] The growth and increase of the church in this region soon required a presiding elder, and Learner Blackman was so assigned in 1804.[121] The eccentric Lorenzo Dow passed hurriedly through Mississippi and Alabama in 1803.[122] His was the first Protestant voice in Alabama, but no preacher was appointed to that section until 1808.[123] Methodism had spread sail; its missionary organization had extended its grasp into the lower section of the Southwest—even into Louisiana by 1805, when E. W. Bowman answered Asbury's call for volunteers.[124] The trip to New Orleans was arduous, and he found the city dirty and in a bad condition morally.[125] John Travis was sent into the new territory of Missouri in 1807.[126]

New names of men destined to carry the burden of Methodism in the new country now appeared on the register of the conferences. Learner Blackman was transferred to the Western Conference in 1803.[127] At the 1804 session Peter Cartwright,[128] a strong and ready man, and James Axley,[129] distinguished by his candor, were admitted on trial and both names later became as familiar as household words.

The Western Conference had grown into one of immense proportions—in 1808 five large districts held within them 19,048 professors of Methodism.[130] The infirmities of age and exposure were preying on the body of Asbury, yet, he pushed on in

---

119 *Journal of the Western Conference,* 1800-1811 (Pt. II of Sweet, *Rise of Methodism*), 86.
120 Bangs, *History of the Methodist Church,* II, 81-82; Jones, *Methodism in Mississippi,* I, 19, 26-28, 60, 66, 67; McTyeire, *History of Methodism,* 500-502; Abel Stevens, *History of American Methodism* (New York, 1867), 405, 407.
121 Finley, *Sketches,* 218-221; McTyeire, *History of Methodism,* 503; Jones, *Methodism in Mississippi,* I, 116; Stevens, *History of Methodism,* 407, 408.
122 Dow, *History of Cosmopolite,* 163-169; B. F. Riley, *History of the Baptists of Alabama* (Birmingham, 1895), 15; Pickett, *History of Alabama,* 472-473.
123 Stevens, *History of Methodism,* 426; Anson West, *A History of Methodism in Alabama* (Nashville, 1892), 27, 28, 38.
124 Redford, *Methodism in Kentucky,* II, 150; McFerrin, *Methodism in Tennessee,* III, 18, 19.
125 See Jones, *Methodism in Mississippi,* I, 145-152.
126 Bangs, *History of Methodism,* II, 191.
127 Young, *Autobiography,* 218, 220; Carr, *Early Times,* 140-146; Finley, *Sketches,* ch. xiv.
128 "Peter Cartwright," *American Historical Record,* I (1872), 567.
129 For sketches of Axley see Redford, *Methodism in Kentucky,* II, 450-457; Cartwright, *Autobiography,* 93-94; Finley, *Sketches,* 231-245.
130 *Minutes,* I, 169, 171.

THE CAMP MEETING 33

his work in spite of fever, a chronic cough, and pain-wracking rheumatism. For months his diary had received comments on declining health. "Ah Me! to pant for breath, and unable to walk, kneel or stand up straight to preach, makes public speaking serious work to me."[131] After the death of Bishop Whatcoat in 1806,[132] and the return of Bishop Coke to Europe,[133] the burden of the bishopric was too heavy for a single pair of shoulders. So to this office was elected in 1808 William McKendree, who was better fitted for the task than any other man in the church, and was the first American elevated to that honor.[134] Asbury was highly pleased with the election since McKendree was a protege of his own, and had stepped from the obscurity of the West and triumphed over the opposition coming from those churchmen who knew little of McKendree's improvement since he had left the Virginia Conference eight years before.[135] Asbury rejoiced with good reason: "The burden is now borne by two pairs of shoulders instead of one; the care is cast upon two hearts and heads."[136]

In September, 1808, Asbury again went over the mountains to attend the Western Conference, which met at Liberty Hill, near Nashville. On the growth of Nashville, he commented: "This town has greatly improved in eight years. There are several valuable houses built, an elegant court-house, and a college."[137] At this conference one of the seventeen preachers admitted on trial was William Winans, who left an everlasting impression on the church, in spite of the fact that he was a year later reprimanded by Bishop McKendree "for his improper conduct toward the female sex especially his making proposals of marriage in an improper way."[138] Winans was with Governor William H. Harrison at Vincennes when Chief Tecumseh came for an interview concerning the treaty with the Miami Indians.

---
131 Asbury, *Journal*, III, 288, 289.
132 See his obituary. *Minutes*, I, 145-146.
133 For this period of Dr. Coke's life see Drew, *Life of Thomas Coke*, ch. xv.
134 Paine, *William McKendree*, ch. viii; E. R. Hendrix, "The General Conference of 1808," *Meth. Rev.* (Nashville, 1908), LVII, 692-711.
135 H. E. Luccock, Paul Hutchinson, *The Story of Methodism* (Cincinnati, 1926), 276, 277.
136 Asbury, *Journal*, III, 280.
137 *Ibid.*, III, 290.
138 For others admitted at this conference see *Journal of the Western Conference*, 142, 161.

Winans' last appearance in the North was at the General Conference of 1844 in New York, at which time the Southern church seceded. As a slaveholding preacher, he took an active part in the controversy, and next to Peter Cartwright, who remained with the parent church, was the most "unique" man at the meeting.[139] Another strong figure of this period was Marcus Lindsey who entered the traveling connection in 1810. Within a year he was given missionary work on the Big Sandy River—a region famed as the refuge of the horse-thief, gambler, and counterfeiter. Lindsey faced his difficulty without fearing danger, and won many to the church. In later years it was Lindsey who was instrumental in the conversion of the negro John Stewart, who went as the first missionary to the Wyandot Indians.[140]

Such representative men formed the backbone of the expanding church.

---

139 Redford, *Methodism in Kentucky,* II, 38, 47.
140 See Finley, *Sketches,* ch. xxx.

CHAPTER III

THE CIRCUIT RIDER AMONG FRONTIER FOLK

A picture of the midwestern frontier in the late eighteenth and early nineteenth centuries is in no wise accurate or complete unless the itinerant Methodist preacher is placed in the immediate foreground. So ardent was the early preacher in the pursuit of his labor that he waited neither upon the manner nor the means of his going. His activity was as mobile as the fluctuating edge of the frontier. It cannot be said that he followed the wagon treks—in truth, he preceded them.[1] A preacher was a pioneer; he had pushed into the new territory along with the hundreds of other restless spirits; he was on hand at every house raising, corn husking, and tree felling; he was present at the weddings, births, and deaths. Being one of the same class as those to whom he was to minister, he had, by his own nature and social status, a perfect understanding of pioneer habits, feelings, and prejudices.[2]

The unified itinerant system of the Methodist Church was exactly suited to a wide-flung population in a new country.[3] The circuit rider was given a territory with a circumference of four hundred or five hundred miles[4] and told to cover it as quickly and efficiently as possible, visiting every settlement and attending to both community and individual needs; and when finished to start over again. Well might the presiding elder have set each itinerant on his way with the injunction: "Take no thought for your life, what ye shall eat, or what ye shall drink; nor yet for your body, what ye shall put on."[5] A year's

---

1 Anderson, "Heroes of Tennessee Methodism," *Tenn. Conf. Jour.*, 1912, p. 107. Two highly interesting personal accounts of circuit riders of a later period are Edward Eggleston, *The Circuit Rider: A Tale of the Heroic Age* (New York, 1893) and Corra Harris, *A Circuit Rider's Wife* (Philadelphia, 1910). Dr. Philip Lindsley, President of the University of Nashville and a contemporary of the period, has said that the uneducated Baptist and Methodist preachers did not lead the upper classes. Le Roy J. Halsey (ed.), *The Works of Philip Lindsley, D. D.* (3 vols., New York, 1866), I, 442-443.
2 Hamilton, *Men and Manners in America*, 394.
3 W. A. McSwain, "Philosophy of Methodist Itineracy," *Meth. Rev.* (Nashville, 1891), X, 120-130.
4 Gewehr, "Factors in the Expansion of Methodism," *Journal of Religion*, VIII (1928), 103-104; Finley, *Autobiography*, 193, 351; Cartwright, *Autobiography*, 64; Finley, *Sketches*, 41. An interesting account of the circuit rider is that by W. W. Sweet, "The Coming of the Circuit Rider Across the Mountains," *Miss. Valley Hist. Rev.*, IX (1922-1923), 271-282.
5 Matthew, vi, 25.

salary of $9.50[6] presupposes a complete reliance on the Lord. Equipped with horse, saddle and bags, a change of clothing, Bible, and 'trusty rifle[7] the circuit rider set out to meet danger and hardship and to labor with zeal and courage. Frequently he rode twenty or thirty miles without seeing a house, and when one was finally found it afforded no better accommodation than could be imagined in a one room cabin, twelve by fourteen, already running over with a man and wife, and many children—frequently fifteen or twenty—"for Providence is bountiful on the frontier in this matter,"[8] and a dog and chickens when the weather was bad.[9] If there was no extra bed the preacher was placed in front of the fire on a rug, which, as a rule, was so full of fleas that a clean plank was preferable.[10] It is not surprising that Bascom chose to spend the night couched in a hollow log.[11]

Generally the preacher was cordially welcomed into the home. His arrival was of high moment, and with genuine hospitality the host offered his coarse fare of wild meat, and cornbread or hominy.[12] Yet occasionally from the more prosperous class the preacher met with a cold refusal. James Axley once sought a night's lodging at the house of a widow, but was straightway informed "that she entertained no such cattle." Axley, however, persuaded her by a song to relent, and the result was that he spent the night in comfort.[13]

Dawn found the rider again on his way, weather being no hindrance in his procedure. "There is nothing out today but crows and Methodist preachers"[14] grew into a proverbial saying. With a circuit which held from twenty-five to thirty appointments[15] it is rather amazing that even Monday was allowed for a

---

6 C. B. Galloway, "Thomas Griffin: A Boanerges of the Early Southwest," Mississippi Historical Society *Publications* VII (1903), 159.
7 A. H. Redford, *Life and Times of H. H. Kavanaugh* (Nashville, 1884), 87; Wright, *Hawkers and Walkers*, 152; Redford, *Methodism in Kentucky*, II, 354.
8 W. H. Milburn, *The Rifle, Axe and Saddle Bags* (New York, 1857), 65.
9 *Ibid.*, pp. xvii-xviii, 56-67.
10 Bangs, *History of the Methodist Church*, I, 272. See a description of a frontier lodging-house in Asbury, *Journal*, III, 131.
11 Henkle, *Life of Bascom*, 70.
12 Finley, *Autobiography*, 69, 74, 297; Cotterill, *Pioneer Kentucky*, 246; Henkle, *Life of Bascom*, 58; Finley, *Sketches*, 207-208; Smith, *History of Kentucky*, 391; A. B. Hart (ed.), *National Expansion*, 1783-1845 (New York, 1901), 464-465, quoted from Morris Birkbeck, *Notes on a Journey in America from the Coast of Virginia to the Territory of Illinois*.
13 Jones, *Methodism in Mississippi*, I, 445-446.
14 Gewehr, "Factors in the Expansion of Methodism," *Journal of Religion*, VIII (1928), 103.
15 Brunson, *Western Pioneer*, I, 180.

rest day. True, it was usually taken up with the washing of clothes.[16] The amount of territory over which the itinerant traveled evinces the assiduity with which he labored. In 1801 two preachers were assigned to the Cumberland Circuit which was six hundred miles around, and lay partly in Kentucky and partly in Tennessee.[17] Finley, immediately upon admission (1809) to the traveling connection, was assigned a circuit of 475 miles.[18] John B. McFerrin, a tender youth of twenty, was assigned (1827) to a perilous circuit among the Cherokees which held in its circumference of four hundred miles portions of Alabama, Tennessee, and Georgia.[19] Francis Asbury, although a bishop, was the complete expression and embodiment of the Western missionary; he crossed the Alleghenies sixty-two times, and the sum total of his travels would circle the globe nine times.[20] Other preachers devoted themselves no less devotedly to their duty. Bascom, young in the service, covered three thousand miles from November, 1814, to August, 1815, and preached to four hundred congregations.[21]

At each station the circuit rider worked with the local or lay minister who conducted the work during the former's absence. The local preachers were of invaluable service in time of revivals, regularly conducted the Sunday Class Meetings, and were "ever attentive to the Macedonian cry."[22] The arrival of the preacher was usually an occasion for renewed religious fervor;[23] yet, occasionally after a hard ride of twenty-five to fifty miles the itinerant would find an empty meetinghouse to greet him.[24]

---

16 Brooks, *Life and Times*, 111.
17 Cartwright, *Autobiography*, 36.
18 Finley, *Autobiography*, 193-194.
19 O. P. Fitzgerald, *John B. McFerrin* (Nashville, 1888), 62-69. In 1809 the Kentucky District extended from the headwaters of the Kentucky River to the mouths of the two Sandys—a distance of five hundred miles. Mitchell Hall, *Johnson County Kentucky, A History of the County, and Genealogy of Its People up to the Year 1927* (2 vols., Louisville, 1928), I, 324. John Kelly, a preacher in East Tennessee, had to carry flour 150 miles in order to have bread for sacrament. Jewell, *Methodism in Arkansas*, 69.
20 Tipple, *Francis Asbury*, 287; C. C. Jarrell, *Methodism on the March* (Nashville, 1924), 113. For the extent of Wesley's evangelistic tours see C. R. Brown, *The Larger Faith* (Boston, 1923), 24.
21 Henkle, *Life of Bascom*, 80-81. For this service Bascom received $12.10.
22 David Wilson, "Local Preachers," *Meth. Rev.* (Nashville, 1882), IV, 705-712; Finley, *Sketches*, 62; Young, *Autobiography*, 77.
23 See Seldes, *The Stammering Century*, 45-47, for a highly interesting description of the psychology attendant upon the preacher's arrival.
24 Henkle, *Life of Bascom*, 46.

In good weather the local meetinghouse was used for the preaching services; however, only a few of the churches were suitable for winter use. The Lebanon (Kentucky) Circuit, one of the oldest in the Western Conference, had ten meetinghouses, and only one of them fit for cold weather. Even that had no chimney.[25] Whenever the weather was too inclement, preaching was done in a cabin or barn,[26] with a marked degree of informality, yet with no tinge of irreverence. On one of Henry Bascom's periodical visits, the congregation had just assembled when a yelp of a dog was heard, and the next minute a bear was seen to run past the meetinghouse. Immediately every man of the congregation followed in the chase. Bascom, seeing his congregation gone, and being swift on foot, was soon ahead of all his people and but a little in the rear of the dogs. After the bear was killed and dragged back to the cabin, the young preacher gave an uncommonly good sermon, and an interesting class meeting followed.[27] On another occasion Bascom was preaching in a cabin, when in the middle of the services, while the people were listening with deep attention, his host rose from his seat, snatched his gun, hastily went out, fired, returned quietly and seated himself. After the sermon Bascom inquired the meaning of his conduct. "Sir," said the host, "we were entirely out of meat; and it was preventing me from enjoying the sermon, when the Good One sent a flock of wild turkeys this way; I happened to see them, took my gun and killed two at a shot; my mind felt easy and I enjoyed the remainder of the sermon with perfect satisfaction."[28]

Game shooting, however, was by no means the only interruption which had to be encountered in the process of a sermon. Enthusiasm and attention frequently lapsed into apathy and lethargy. Congregations slept no less in the eighteen twenties than a century later. On one occasion while Bascom was preaching a gentleman fell asleep immediately in front of the pulpit,

---

25 Brooks, *Life and Times*, 225. There were other objections to the meetinghouse as seen in the title of an article, "Impure Air in Churches," *Meth. Mag.*, IX (1826), 102-103.
26 Rusk, *Literature of the Frontier*, I, 50. Asbury's *Journal* is replete with descriptions of frontier conditions.
27 Henkle, *Life of Bascom*, 73-77.
28 *Ibid.*, 128.

and about the same time just outside of the window two men began to talk loudly. Each of these circumstances angered him, and, in order to free himself of the nuisance, he turned to the window and addressed the talkers outside, "Gentlemen, I will thank you to speak in a lower tone of voice, or you will disturb my friend who is sleeping here in front of the pulpit."[29] The rebuke was electric in effect.

Frequently rowdies sought to break up a meeting, and the preacher was faced with a delicate situation in the actual preservation of order. In view of this fact the frontier preacher became an instrument of the law. A typical scene is one in which Peter Cartwright, after having unsuccessfully tried to quiet some rowdies who talked and jeered during his sermon, attended to the youngsters in his own muscular way. In telling of this event Cartwright said:

> I stopped trying to preach, and called for a magistrate. There were two on hand, but I saw they were both afraid. I ordered them to take these men in custody, but they said they could not do it. I told them, as I left the stand, to command me to take them and I would do it at the risk of my life .... One of them [rowdies] made a pass at my head with his whip, but I closed in with him and jerked him off the seat. A regular suffle ensued .... We secured about thirty prisoners, and, ... when they were tried every man was fined to the utmost limit of the law.[30]

Nor was this an unusual situation. Rev. Arthur Davis on arriving at a meeting in West Tennessee was met by a band of outlaws who announced that "no d—d Methodist preacher should preach in that house." Completely disregarding the threat Davis preached his sermon, and at the close turned to his adversaries saying, "I am now ready to meet you." So unexpected was this boldness and courage on the part of the preacher that the leader of the group threw down his club and said, "You're my sort of man; ... you shall preach here whenever it may please you to do so, and I will see you do it in peace."[31]

---

29 *Idem.*
30 Cartwright, *Autobiography*, 91-92.
31 J. S. Williams, *Old Times in West Tennessee, Reminiscences—Semi-historic—of Pioneer Life and the Early Emigrant Settlers in the Big Hatchie Country* (Memphis, 1873), 62-63. For other examples of Davis' manner of handling situations see Redford, *Western Cavaliers*, 52-58.

The preacher was frequently called on to act as a servant of the law in order to keep public conduct within restraint. Lawyers and officers were scarce in the outposts of settlement; the profession of law was considered one of rascality;[32] and, furthermore, the frontiersman often disregarded law and government.[33] Justice was meagerly meted out, and little improvement in the situation had been made since 1800, at which time a congressional record report revealed that in "three Western counties there had been but one court having cognizance of crimes in five years."[34]

The need for medical advice and service was so urgent that many preachers of these times took up the practice of medicine without any license.[35] A. L. P. Green extensively combined medical practice with his preaching; he carried as part of his regular equipment a stock of pills and powders for sickly babies and rheumatic old folk.[36] The absence of doctors in the West encouraged the use of herbal remedies which were brewed in almost every kitchen. Only in extreme labor at childbirth was outside aid called, and then it was usually the local midwife who came with her scissors and conjuring power. Bishop Asbury tells of a home remedy which he took when suffering from general debility. A morning dose was "made of one quart of hard cider, one hundred nails, a handful of black snake roots, one handful of fennel seed, one handful of wormwood." This was boiled strong, until condensed "from a quart to a pint."[37]

Now was the glowing opportunity and time for the successful launching of a patent medicine, which would be a remedy equally effective for many ailments. And to the shrewd and crafty Lorenzo Dow came the idea of capitalizing the formula of an old English friend, Dr. Paul Johnson. In November, 1820, by official action of the United States Patent Office, "Lorenzo

---

32 For one of the best commentaries on the politics of the time see J. W. M. Breazeale, *Life as It Is, or, Manners and Things in General* (Knoxville, 1842).
33 J. T. Adams, *The Epic of America* (Boston, 1931), 49.
34 W. A. Candler, *Great Revivals and the Great Republic* (Nashville, 1904), 155.
35 In 1817 the Ohio Conference expelled one of its members, Lemuel Lane, on three charges, one of which was for "Practicing medicine without sufficient knowledge [and] practicing the science of midwifery without skill." *Journals of the Ohio Annual Conference*, 1812-1826 (Pt. II of W. W. Sweet, *Circuit Rider Days Along the Ohio*, Cincinnati, 1923), 154.
36 Green, *Life and Papers of A. L. P. Green*, 109.
37 Quoted by Bennett, "Pioneer Methodism in Virginia," *Meth. Rev.* (Nashville, 1888), V, 95. For other remedies used by Asbury, see his *Journal*, I, 142; II, 148, 347, 349; III, 88.

Dow's Family Medicine" made its appearance. An early advertisement of his remedy bears all the personal and testimonial elements required by high-powered salesmanship and advertising of the present business age. It testified that:

> We, the Subscribers, having made a fair use (in our families) of Lorenzo Dow's Family Medicine, do certify, That it is very gentle and sure in its operation as a cathartic and that it possesses a peculiar quality to remove obstructions in the stomach and bowels, and in carrying off bad humours. And that it is well adopted to females in a debilitated or declining state, forasmuch as it does not weaken the patient (although taken frequently) but rather restores the stomach to a proper tone by assisting the digestion, and thereby exciting the appetite, etc.[38]

Such constant and rigorous duties outside of the actual business of preaching developed an energetic and zealous ministry, yet it provided scant time for cultural achievement.[39] Fortunately the traveling preacher had but few sermons to prepare. His extra-Biblical sources were generally no more than Wesley's *Articles of Religion, Notes on the New Testament,* and *Scriptural Doctrine of Predestination, Election and Reprobation.*[40] Of course some of the more studious ministers read more widely. Francis Asbury, at the head of these exceptions, read in addition to the above: Newton's *Divinity* and *Dissertations,* Osterwald's *Christian Theology,* the works of Flouch and Norris, Prideaux on *The Connection of the History of the Old and New Testament,* Ogden and Barclay, and hundreds of others covering every phase of life.[41] The lack of time for reading plus an already meager education produced a clergy which exhorted in a simple, direct, and forceful language, unadorned by rhetorical flourishes, and in a style unfettered by manuscript.[42] As late as 1821 Peter Cartwright believed that "there was not a single literary man" among the 280 preachers traveling in what he termed the "far

---

38 Sellers, *Lorenzo Dow,* 200, 202.
39 Rusk, *Literature of the Frontier,* I, 50.
40 Cutshall, *Training of the Ministry,* 18.
41 *Ibid.,* 46. Tipple (*Francis Asbury,* 92-102) gives the titles of many of the books which Asbury read.
42 Cleveland, *The Great Revival,* 110-111.

west."⁴³ The fact that Rev. John Lyle preached for two hours and twenty minutes with "almost no time for reflection or meditation"⁴⁴ suggests that liberty and freedom were not denied the preacher.

The religion preached was not elaborate with much doctrine, for it was essentially suited to the rugged frontier. "Its essential democracy, its fiery and restless energy of spirit and the wide play it gave to individual initiative, all tended to make it peculiarly congenial to a hardy and virile folk, democratic to the core, prizing individual independence above all earthly possessions and engaged in the rough and stern work of conquering a continent."⁴⁵ The doctrine of individual responsibility, no doubt, had the greatest appeal; a great satisfaction was found in the close relationship which was preached as existing between God and man.⁴⁶ This must have been a comforting tenet to those who lived so remote from human contacts. On the other hand, a sharp tongue was perhaps as strong a force for conversion as any point of doctrine. The congregation at whom was hurled the accusation "You are a moving mass of putrefaction," no doubt, was convinced that it was "the butt-cut of sin."⁴⁷

The preacher had a powerful device in his hand beyond creed and liturgy in effectiveness. Methodism from its initiation had hymns that contained every phase of Christian theology,⁴⁸ and in turn served as the chief means of indoctrinating the masses in the principles for which Methodism stood. "After the scriptures," so evaluated James Martineau, a Unitarian preacher, "the Wesley hymn-book appears to me the grandest instrument of popular culture that Christendom has ever produced."⁴⁹ Peo-

---

43 Cartwright, *Autobiography,* 197. Timothy Flint who traveled extensively in the west was convinced that the ill-trained Methodist preacher who spoke the native dialect and entered into the feelings of the people could succeed where more polished ministers would fail. Flint, *The History and Geography of the Mississippi Valley* (2 vols., Cincinnati, 1832), I, 146. As late as 1830 and 1831 Dr. Samuel Wait, a Baptist clergyman, while traveling over the State of North Carolina was impressed with the illiteracy of Baptist preachers. At a large assembly of Baptist ministers, Dr. Wait found only five college graduates. C. B. Williams, *A History of the Baptists in North Carolina* (Raleigh, 1901), 85.
44 Lyle, *Diary,* 50.
45 Quoted by L. A. Weigle, *American Idealism* (New Haven, 1928), 150.
46 Sweet, *Rise of Methodism,* 14-15.
47 Williams, *Old Times,* 65-66.
48 Candler, *Great Revivals,* 110.
49 Quoted by Weigle, *American Idealism,* 149; here Weigle reproduces pages 334 and 335 of *A Collection of Hymns for the Use of the Methodist Church* (1822). See C. F. Price, "A Century of Methodist Song," *Christian Advocate,* CI (1926), 1139-1141.

ple always have found great pleasure in song, and a theme expressed in rhyme and rhythm penetrated the outer crust of reserve and touched the emotions in a way which the spoken word never accomplished. Such verses as

> There is a land of pure delight,
> Where saints immortal reign;
> Infinite day excludes the night,
> And pleasures banish pain.
>
> Sweet fields beyond the swelling flood,
> Stand dressed in living green;
> So to the Jews old Canaan stood,
> While Jordan roll'd between.
>
> Could we but climb where Moses stood,
> And view the landscape o'er;
> Not Jordan's stream nor death's cold flood,
> Should fright us from the shore.[50]

provided the motivation for large gatherings where hundreds were swept by emotion. The camp meetings afforded a prolific source for "spirituals," and in turn furnished a magnificent demonstration of the power of music.[51]

Uneducated and even illiterate as most of the frontier preachers were, their interest in the advancement of education is indicative of their acumen as to all frontier needs. Letters from the older preachers bear evidence of their deep concern in a more learned clergy.[52] William H. Milburn once wrote, "I have known many a man who could not construct a half dozen sentences grammatically to bestow half of his yearly stipend to establish an institution of learning."[53] Augusta College, Bethel Academy, and Cokesbury College arose as living monuments to the efforts of these sacrificing men in Tennessee and Kentucky.[54]

---

[50] Hymn CCCXIX in *The Methodist Pocket Hymn-Book Revised and Improved Designed as a Constant Companion for the Pious of all Denominations* (New York, 1813). This book is four by three inches and contains 350 hymns.
[51] See E. E. Harper, "The Music and Worship of Methodism," *Christian Advocate*, CI (1926), 1138-1139; E. R. Hendrix, "The Evolution of the Methodist Hymnal," *Meth. Rev.* (Nashville, 1906), LV, 3-18.
[52] See "Review of Rev. H. B. Bascom's Inaugural Address," *Meth. Mag.*, XI (1828), 147-151.
[53] Milburn, *Rifle, Axe and Saddle Bags*, 57.
[54] A. W. Cummings, *The Early Schools of Methodism*, (New York, 1886).

The way of the circuit rider rarely ever served as a path to personal glory. The entire life of an itinerant was charged with hardships, abnegations, and sacrifices. From his acceptance of "the call," his whole time and entire effort were devoted to the duty he had assumed. He was a man who spent most of his time for others; yet, within himself, lived apart. Even his appearance marked him as a clergyman. A child could recognize a parson's attire of long, double breasted coat[55] of dingy black, with short breeches and long stockings. Hair parted in the middle and hanging long to the shoulders[56] accentuated "his chaste and sanctified look" and added to the naturally haggard and pale face caused by scant food and frequent exposure. Brooks told of a most singular meeting he had with a Methodist preacher.

> I had been accustomed to see preachers, but this one looked so different from any other I had ever seen; . . . he seemed to be an inhabitant of eternity, though a man on earth. Never, never, shall I forget his looks. I felt my strength give way as he passed me, and I like to have fallen to the ground.[57]

Not all of the preachers, however, were so ethereal. Prior to 1825 when the temperance movement gained strength, many were dram drinkers,[58] and a large number were habitual chewers of tobacco.[59] Conferences dismissed or expelled several itinerants for drinking,[60] and for "immoral"[61] or "improper"[62] conduct. A conference temporarily suspended from the ministry Moses Floyd, a missionary in Mississippi, after he had eloped with a young woman. It charged him with having "lowered the standard of the Methodist ministry in the public mind."[63] The same conference tried and reprimanded E. W. Bowman "for wearing weapons calculated to inspire terror and for threatening what he would do."[64] Some of the preachers were cunning at bargaining

---

55 Brooks, *Life and Times*, 103, 104.
56 Sweet, *Circuit Rider Days in Indiana*, 7, 34.
57 Brooks, *Life and Times*, 9.
58 Cartwright, *Autobiography*, 137-138, 212-213.
59 Wright, *Hawkers and Walkers*, 150.
60 Cartwright, *Autobiography*, 185; Herbert Asbury, "The Father of Prohibition," *American Mercury*, IX (1926), 345.
61 *Minutes*, I, 66, 73.
62 *Ibid.*, I, 49, 54.
63 Price, *Holston Methodism*, I, 412.
64 *Journal of the Western Conference*, 203.

and were such good judges of horse flesh that they were "a little dangerous at the trade."[65] Among these preachers there were no Chesterfields in manner; crude and uncouth were the adjectives which were generally applicable. Few of them knew anything of polished life.[66] A typical story is one told concerning James Axley, who, when being entertained by the governor of Ohio,[67] took a leg of chicken "in his fingers, and ate it in that way; when he had got the flesh from the bone, he turned round and whistled for the little lap-dog, and threw the bone down on the carpet." When later reproved by Peter Cartwright for such conduct he burst into tears and said, "Why did you not tell me better? I didn't know any better."[68]

To enter the ministry was equivalent to taking the vows of poverty and chastity.[69] Few preachers ever courted or thought of marriage until they had traveled for six years.[70] Marriage was openly discouraged by the bishops;[71] and few men had the courage to expose a woman to the privations and hardships of an itinerant's life.

> Such was the prejudice that existed in the Church, at that day, against married preachers, that it was almost out of the question for any man to continue work if he had a wife. They were not exactly obliged to take the Popish vow of celibacy, but it almost amounted to the same thing; and there being such a high example for single life, as exhibited in the cases of the bishops, if a preacher married he was looked upon almost as a heretic who had denied the faith . . . . We recollect that within the last twenty years, in the Ohio conference, young men have been discontinued who married within two years, though there was nothing else against them.[72]

Certainly a married clergy was no plan of the early general conferences, for no salary provision was made for a wife or family before 1792. At this date an allowance of sixty-four

---

[65] Milburn, *Rifle, Axe and Saddle Bags*, 56; E. E. Hoss, *David Morton: A Biography* (Nashville, 1916), 56.
[66] For the attitude of a foreign traveler toward western Methodist clergymen see Flint, *Letters from America*, 196.
[67] Edward Tiffin, a Methodist local preacher.
[68] Cartwright, *Autobiography*, 93-94.
[69] Wright, *Hawkers and Walkers*, 150.
[70] Brooks, *Life and Times*, 111.
[71] Finley, *Sketches*, 49-50. See the reasons of Asbury for celibacy. *Journal*, III, 143.
[72] Finley, *Sketches*, 180-181.

dollars was made to the preacher's wife, sixteen dollars for each child under six, and twenty-four dollars for each over six and under eleven years, in addition to expenses. Eight years later the preacher's salary was increased to the considerable sum of eighty dollars per annum, and the same was granted to his wife; sixteen dollars was provided for each child under seven and for those over that age and under fourteen twenty-four dollars was allowed. By 1816 the salary clause called for one hundred dollars; the allowance for children remained the same.[73] It is not to be understood that these amounts were always collected by the preacher.[74] James Finley evidently failed to receive his salary, for he wrote, "I sold the boots off my feet to purchase provisions with,"[75] and again, "I borrowed a blanket, and wore it instead of a great coat through the winter, and by that means paid my debts."[76] A few weeks of hard riding were enough to wear threadbare the cheap breeches, and on the occurrence of such a misfortune one's pride had no alternative but patches. Bishop Asbury made note of the physical condition of the clergy: "I found the poor preachers indifferently clad, with emaciated bodies and subject to hard fare; but I hope they are rich in faith."[77] In face of such facts the statements made by some writers that the preachers were moderate in dress and habit, that they "did not follow the ever changing fashions of the cut of dress; they remained in the same fashion,"[78] amount to truisms.

Not all of the circuit rider's courage could be consumed in the endurance of hardships, for great dangers lurked within the forest and around every curve of the way. The roads were so treacherous and the streams so difficult to ford that the preacher rarely attempted to travel in a wheeled vehicle.[79] The abundance of wild animals and the presence of Indians made more dangerous the already hazardous journeys. Among the precautions taken

---

73 Bangs, *History of the Methodist Church*, II, 95.
74 Henkle, *Life of Bascom*, 80-81.
75 Finley, *Autobiography*, 194. For lending of horse and payment of quarterage see "Ministerial Support," *Meth. Rev.* (Nashville, 1892), XII, 99.
76 Finley, *Sketches*, 53, 91; Finley, *Autobiography*, 193.
77 Asbury, *Journal*, II, 79.
78 Brooks, *Life and Times*, 103.
79 Asbury and McKendree traveled to the General Conference of 1808 in a thirty-dollar chaise, but had to carry an axe in order to clear the roads of obstructing trees and brush. Annie Barnes, *Scenes in Pioneer Methodism* (2 vols., Nashville, 1892), II, 188.

against Indian attacks was the customary advertisement of a regular meeting place, from which a sufficient number of preachers could proceed to a conference under mutual protection. One indiscreet group, however, started to the Kentucky Conference of 1794 without a guard, and had proceeded scarcely a mile before they were met by a band of Indians, who by quick work rode on with scalps as trophies.[80]

In this way the itinerant assumed his task: he went

> through storms of wind, hail, snow, and rain; climbed hills and mountains, traversed valleys, plunged through swamps, swam swollen streams, lay out all night, wet, weary, and hungry, held his horse by the bridle all night, or tied him to a limb, slept with his saddle blanket for a bed, his saddle or saddle-bags for his pillow, and his old big coat or blanket, if he had any, for a covering. Often he slept in dirty cabins, on earthen floors, before the fire; ate roasting ears for bread, drank butter-milk for coffee, or sage tea for imperial; took, with a heavy zest, deer or bear meat, or wild turkey, for breakfast, dinner, and supper, if he could get it.[81]

In spite of such physical trials the preacher's text was always "Behold the Lamb of God, that taketh away the sins of the world." This was old-fashioned Methodist fare and fortune.[82]

The camp meeting and the circuit rider exerted a profound influence in extending the Methodist Church in the Old Southwest. An increase in church membership and a new devoutness in the Westerner were contributions which were apparent throughout the whole of the frontier regions. Yet, in spite of the activity of the institution and of the individual, not all of the Western people were won to the church. Many remained indifferent to the solemn warnings heard in the camp meeting and preached by the rider on the circuit.

---

[80] Finley, *Sketches*, 37-39.
[81] Cartwright, *Autobiography*, 243. See, also, Redford, *Life of Kavanaugh*, 87. Sometimes the food was not clean. Alfred Brunson once found a cooked frog in a bowl of mush which had been served to him. Brunson, *Western Pioneer*, I, 105.
[82] Cartwright, *Autobiography*, 243. See "Methodist Evangelism," Tipple, *Francis Asbury*, ch. ix; J. E. Edwards, *Life of Rev. John Wesley Childs* (Louisville, 1852), 52.

CHAPTER IV

EARTHQUAKES AND WAR, 1812-1815

As a result of the activity of the circuit rider and his camp meeting device the frontiersman became aware of a partial necessity for religious worship. This sense of consciousness was by no means acute, but lay on the periphery of his mental activities, and, although he perhaps was not aware of its presence, this sensibility was easily intensified with the proper stimulus. It was a state of mind which would be highly susceptible to the effects of natural phenomena.

Nature with its capricious phenomena has ever presented itself to man as an ominous instrument in the hands of a god or gods.[1] Universal law becomes a mere generalization in the presence of unusual events, and every extraordinary thing is then embraced by the sweeping adjective, miraculous. From his first consciousness man has stood aghast at any unusual occurrence in nature—whether it is an over-flowing Nile, a preserving ray of the sun, a falling star, a flash of a comet, a nebulous mass, a stream of lava, or an earth tremor. All are read in the light of supernatural interpositions, and the voice of a Christian god is no less threatening than that of an angry Posiedon. Every strange occurrence is alarming but none quite so terrifying as for the earth, which seems so stable and secure, to quake and tremble under man's feet. In a section frequented by earth tremors the consternation grows less with each recurrence, but in a region so far removed from an active volcano as the Mississippi Valley,[2] the event wrought panic in the minds of the inhabitants of this section.

The settlers of the early 1800's found the region along the Mississippi River rich in a soft loamy soil yielding to immediate cultivation, in streams abounding in fish, and in forests full of game. Thus, with the country offering a solution to its own

---

1 For instances of ancient superstitions, including those caused by earthquakes, see W. E. H. Lecky, *History of European Morals* (2 vols., London, 1911), I, 152-160. For earthquakes as signs of God's wrath, theory of their cause, and effect of terror produced by them see A. D. White, *A History of the Warfare of Science with Theology in Christendom* (2 vols., New York, 1925), I, 197, 327, 331; II, 68

2 See Charles Lyell, *A Second Visit to the United States* (2 vols., London, 1849), II, 230.

riddle of livelihood, the frontiersman rested in content on the adequacy of his section, and feeling no need for divine help, he gave little concern to the matter of religion.[3] Shadows of an approaching war with England produced a greater moral laxity and caused a more marked religious neglect. Yet a hidden danger coming from the very earth that had so generously furnished sustenance was to check this neglect.

Beginning on December 16, 1811, and continuing for weeks, the Central Mississippi region was rocked by a series of earthquakes, the like of which the white man has never known before nor since in that region.[4] Many travelers who were attracted to the area devastated by the quakes have recorded descriptions of the unusual event.[5] The journal of Lorenzo Dow contains a letter from Eliza Bryan who had lived in the very center of the disturbance, New Madrid, Missouri, in which she reported that from December 16, 1811, until February 7, 1812, there was a series of continual shocks, sometimes several a day, but the concussion which took place in the early morning of the latter day was so violent that it was known as the "hard shock." The terror of the early morning darkness was augmented by sulphurated fumes and the deafening thunder from the shifting and splitting earth. A telling description is found in portions of Eliza Bryan's letter:

> The Mississippi first seemed to recede from its banks, and its waters gathered up like a mountain . . . then rising fifteen or twenty feet perpendicularly, and expanding, as it were, at the same moment, the banks were overflowed with a retrograde current, rapid as a torrent . . . . The river falling

---

[3] Cotterill (*Pioneer Kentucky*, 22) said, "After the most liberal estimate is made, the admission must still be made that two-thirds of the population of Kentucky in 1792 were content to live without the folds of the Church." For interesting sidelights on later religious conditions and reasons for spiritual neglect see Lyle, *Diary* and McAfee, *Life and Times*. Also, see McNemar, *The Kentucky Revival;* Davidson, *The Presbyterian Church in Kentucky;* Cossitt, *Finis Ewing*.

[4] For bibliography of original source material of the New Madrid earthquakes see F. A. Sampson, "The New Madrid and Other Earthquakes in Missouri," *Proceedings of the Mississippi Valley Historical Association*, VI (1912-1913), 218-238. See, also, S. C. Williams, *Beginnings of West Tennessee*, 1541-1841 (Johnson City, Tennessee, 1930), ch. x; and Julia Levering, *Historic Indiana* (New York, 1916), 133-134.

[5] Flint, *Recollections*, 222-225; John Bradbury, *Travels in the Interior of America in the Years* 1809, 1810, *and* 1811 (Thwaites, *Early Western Travels*, V, Cleveland, 1904), 201-210; Thomas Nuttall, *Journal of Travels in the Arkansa Territory During the Year* 1819 (Thwaites, *Early Western Travels*, XIII, Cleveland, 1904), 77-78.

immediately, as rapidly as it had risen, receded within its banks again with such violence that it took with it whole groves of young cottonwood trees, which hedged its borders .... The surface of hundreds of acres was, from time to time, covered over, of various depths, by the sand which issued from fissures, which were made in great numbers all over this country ... and lately it has been discovered that a lake was formed on the opposite side of the Mississippi, in the Indian Country, upward of one hundred miles in length, and from one to six miles in width, of the depth from ten to fifty feet.[6]

No doubt portions of her description are greatly exaggerated because of her immediate experience in this disaster. The one-hundred-mile lake is reduced in reality to fourteen and one-half miles long, and four and one-half miles wide and bears the name Reelfoot Lake in West Tennessee. The destruction caused by these quakes was tremendous and far-reaching. Reports of tremors came from Canada, New Orleans, Detroit, Washington, and even Boston. The section shaken hardest lay along the Mississippi River between parallels thirty-six and thirty-seven. The river bank at New Madrid caved in, taking with it the greater part of the town; while farther down the river Caruthersville was completely destroyed. The loss of life was small because people fled for safety to the hills nearby.[7] Intermittent vibrations did not cease for over a year from the date of the first shock. "During the succeeding three months 1,874 shocks were recorded of which 8 were violently severe, 10 very severe, and 35 generally alarming."[8]

It is not surprising that these superstitious and credulous people read the wrath of God in every quake that shook the earth so incessantly for three months. "Respect for signs and omens constituted a conspicuous feature of their mental characteristics, and made them easily moved by shrewd interposition of natural phenomena."[9] Many and varied theories arose as to

---

6 Lorenzo Dow, *The Dealings of God, Man and Devil, As Exemplified in the Life, Experiences and Travels of Lorenzo Dow* (Cincinnati, 1858), 155-156.

7 W. A. Nelson, "Reelfoot—An Earthquake Lake," *National Geographic Magazine*, XLV (1924), 106-107.

8 M. L. Fuller, "Our Greatest Earthquakes," *Popular Science Monthly*, LXIX (1916), 78. See, also, Fuller's article "The New Madrid Earthquake," in the United States *Geological Survey Bulletin*, 1912, no. 404.

9 Perrin, *History of Kentucky*, 219.

the cause of the disturbance. One man expressed the belief that the earth had been caught in the tail of a comet and was trying to dislodge itself.[10] Another feared that the shocks had been caused by the reaction of chemicals on copper that he had buried in order that it might undergo a process that would fit it for use in making counterfeit money.[11] To others, less rational, each tremor was clearly a sign of the termination of the earth, the end of man's probation, and they at once "became alarmed and fled, many to Christ, but more into the Church for refuge."[12]

"It was a time of great horror to sinners."[13]

Histories and diaries of this period furnish some incidents which depict this sudden consciousness of guilt. One extreme tremor caused fourteen sin-hardened men to fall groaning to the floor and to become unconscious from terror.[14] Preaching was interrupted by shrieks of alarm when cupboard doors were seen to fly open.[15] One man grew so alarmed over the hue of his sins and the nearness of the Judgment Day that he sent for the local preacher, urging him to come immediately, for his case was the "worse case in all the country; that it was the most difficult of any as he had been a very bad man."[16]

Everywhere the landslidings were to the people reminders of their "blackslidings," and in great fear they sought a means of expiation. Many sought grace with religious fervor and devotion; others merely rushed into the church seeking a safety from the potency of these phenomena.[17] "Preachers were everywhere implored to preach and to pray for the people; there was a great awakening among the inhabitants, while men's hearts failed them, and their knees smote together in fear."[18] In answer to their call, preachers flocked to the devastated areas to gather in the repentant and to experience the profound sensation of a divine manifestation. These preachers were not always able to with-

---
10 Bradbury, *Travels in America*, 209.
11 J. H. Burrows, "History of Giles County," undated newspaper clipping in the Tennessee State Library.
12 Jewell, *Methodism in Arkansas*, 27.
13 Finley, *Autobiography*, 238.
14 Sellers, *Lorenzo Dow*, 169.
15 Finley, *Autobiography*, 238.
16 Jewell, *Methodism in Arkansas*, 26.
17 Jones, *Methodism in Mississippi*, I, 217; Lewis Collins, *History of Kentucky* (Louisville, 1877), 282-284; Jewell, *Methodism in Arkansas*, 27; Flint, *Recollections*, 222-225; Sellers, *Lorenzo Dow*, 169-170.
18 McFerrin, *Methodism in Tennessee*, II, 263.

stand the temptation to use the power so suddenly put in their hands, and many anecdotes are told "which indicate that much of their remarkable power was due to a somewhat unscrupulous play upon the credulity of unsophisticated minds."[19] James B. Finley was once staying at a cabin where there were many sin-hardened men. When a hard shock set the earth to trembling, he jumped to a table and cried, "For the great day of His wrath is come, and who shall be able to stand?"[20]

The Western Conference of the Methodist Church enjoyed a most fruitful year. The increase in church membership tells its own story with convincing evidence; yet, in the church history of this period little reference and less consideration is given to this source of church additions. Peter Cartwright, one of the few church historians who gave space to the earthquakes, recognized them as evangelical factors, and wrote: "Though many were sincere and stood firm, yet there were hundreds that no doubt joined from sore fright."[21] According to another participant, "The Lord had not only terribly shaken the earth, but had also mercifully shaken the hearts of the people."[22]

It is to be doubted that the personality of any great preacher in this section accounts for the large gain in membership. A wide-sweeping revival did not win these converts. The sudden increase in church membership may be attributed to the fright and alarm which the people experienced as the result of the earthquakes. It must be admitted that the itinerants "struck while the iron was hot"; thus, they minimized their own labor since the people had already created their own psychological moment of appeal. Concerning this matter James B. Finley wrote: "It contributed greatly to increase the interest on the subject of religion. Multitudes who previously paid no attention . . . now flocked out to meeting . . . . The number of converts was great, and the work extended almost everywhere."[23]

In the Methodist Church the Western Conference in 1811 was composed of the whole of Tennessee, Kentucky, and con-

---

19 Perrin, *History of Kentucky*, 219.
20 Quoted by Sellers, *Lorenzo Dow*, 169.
21 Cartwright, *Autobiography*, 181.
22 Paine, *William McKendree*, 240.
23 Finley, *Autobiography*, 239.

tiguous sections of Mississippi, Arkansas, Illinois, Indiana, Ohio, and western Virginia,[24] nearly all of whch lay in the seismical region of 1811 and 1812. In 1811 the Western Conference had a total membership of 30,741. This same territory (divided in 1812 into the Tennessee and Ohio conferences) at the next conference reported 45,983, a net gain of 15,242,[25] which was an increase of more than fifty per cent,[26] while in the years of 1811, 1812, and 1813, the whole of the country outside of the West increased its membership from 157,419 to 164,616, and to 168,324—additions of 7,197 and 3,708 respectively.[27] A study of diagram "A" shows with graphical clarity the sudden increase in membership in the Western Conference during the period in which the earthquakes were occurring as compared with the ten years preceding and following 1812.[28] Membership for the whole of the country during the same years is indicated in diagram "B".

At the General Conference of May, 1812, the Western Conference was divided into the Ohio and Tennessee conferences. The boundaries of the latter, according to the *Journal,* "shall enclose Holston, Nashville, Cumberland, Wabash, Illinois, and Mississippi Districts";[29] and the Ohio Conference embraced the Ohio, Muskingum, Miami, Kentucky, and Salt River districts.[30] Geographically the Tennessee districts included southwestern Virginia, all of Tennessee, and all of the settled portions of Illinois, Missouri, Arkansas, Mississippi, Louisiana, and part of Alabama; while the Ohio extended from western Pennsylvania, New York, and Virginia, through Ohio, the lower part of Indiana, and half of Kentucky.[31]

---

24 See map of the Western Conference. Sweet, *Rise of Methodism,* 34.
25 *Minutes,* I, 211-219.
26 See Paine, *William McKendree,* 240.
27 *Minutes,* I, 197-211. A reference to the *Minutes* reveals the fact that I have used the conference year for the nation as a whole, whereas I have given the Western membership from the *Minutes* of one year later. This is because of the conference dates; for example, of the eight conferences of American Methodism in 1812, all held their sessions in the year 1812 except the Western and the South Carolina, those having been held in October and December, 1811. Thus the statistics for the earthquake period were not recorded in the *Minutes* for 1812 but in those for 1813.
28 *Ibid.,* I, 104-409.
29 *Journals of the General Conference,* I, 108-109.
30 Redford, *Methodism in Kentucky,* II, 244.
31 Sweet, *Circuit Rider Days Along the Ohio,* 27-28.

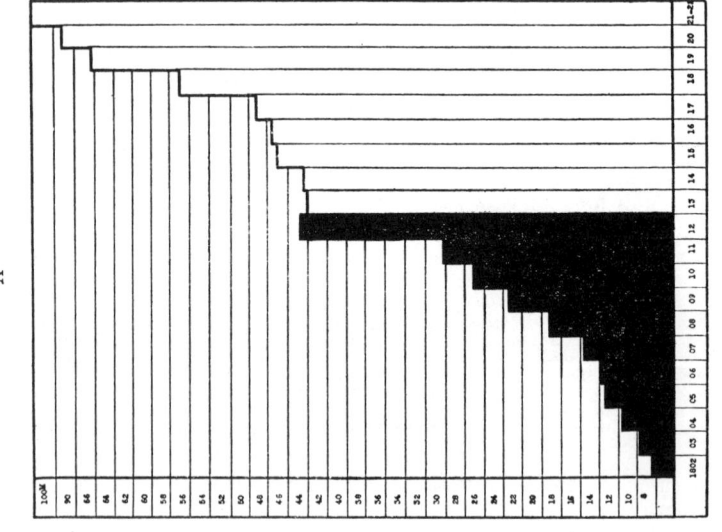

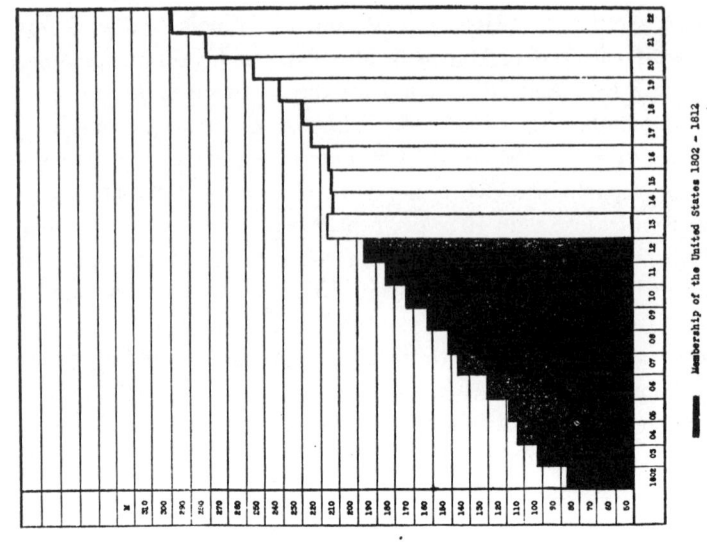

EARTHQUAKES AND WAR

According to the *Minutes* the first session of the Tennessee Conference was to have been held at Fountain Head in Sumner County, Tennessee, on November 1, 1812; but for some cause it did not commence until November 12.[32] Bishops Asbury and McKendree were both present. The former wrote in his *Journal*:

> We opened our conference in great peace; forty deacons were ordained and ten elders; the travelling and local ministry amounts to sixty-two; the net increase, after allowing for death and removal, two. I am comforted with an increase of eight thousand in the Tennessee Conference. If we meet the Mississippi Conference as appointed, in November, 1813, we shall have gone entirely around the United States in forty-two years.[33]

The Tennessee Conference reported a membership, white and colored, of 22,899, distributed as follows:

	Whites	Colored
Holston District	5794	541
Cumberland District	4365	527
Nashville District	5131	601
Wabash District	2911	282
Mississippi District	1067	240
Illinois District	1365	75
	20633	2266[34]

The church was growing in East Tennessee and Asbury noted a perceptible progress when he went to North Carolina by the way of Knoxville after the 1812 Tennessee Conference. Of the good effects he wrote: "God hath wrought upon the vilest of the vile in the fork of Pigeon and Broad Rivers, and He will yet do wonders."[35]

Both Asbury and McKendree were at the first Ohio Conference which convened in the fall of 1812 at Chillicothe. Asbury was busy with the conference affairs; yet, because of the growing weakness of the elder bishop, McKendree presided over the ses-

---
[32] McFerrin, *Methodism in Tennessee*, II, 173; Redford, *Methodism in Kentucky*, II, 265; Price, *Holston Methodism*, II, 166.
[33] Asbury, *Journal*, III, 399-400. He said further: "but there will be other states: well, God will raise up men to make and to meet conferences in them also . . . ." *Ibid.*, III, 400.
[34] *Minutes*, I, 227.
[35] Asbury, *Journal*, III, 400. See, also, Luccock, *The Story of Methodism*, 250.

sions.[36] The membership of the Ohio Conference was reported from each district as follows:

	Whites	Colored
Ohio District	2847	10
Kentucky District	4317	247
Muskingum District	2909	41
Salt River District	3482	213
Miami District	9168	50
	22723	561[37]

The report of the Committee of Temporal Business revealed more "deficiencies" than any other item. Only twenty out of sixty-three registered members of this conference had received their full year's pay of eighty dollars if single, or one hundred and sixty if married.[38]

Between the meetings of the General Conference and the Tennessee and Ohio conferences, the beginning of the war with England suddenly checked the spiritual development of the West. As a result of the war the church lost much it had gained through earthquakes and general religious zeal. It found itself immediately supplanted by new interests. The martial spirit flamed up in every community; the church "continually declined in numerical strength."[39] People became so much taken up with politics and war that they lost their zeal in the cause of God.[40] Finley complained that the spirit of belligerency caused many professors to give up religion. "Wars and rumors of war are peculiarly fatal to a mild and peaceful spirit of the Gospel."[41] A letter to McKendree from Dr. Henry Wilkins of Baltimore, dated August 11, 1813, indicates the pulse in that vicinity. "There is no political division in our church, though great coldness, and few conversions."[42] Within a year the Tennessee and Ohio conferences lost respectively 984 and 1,899 members.[43] This

---
36 Tipple, *Francis Asbury*, 290; Sweet, *Circuit Rider Days Along the Ohio*, 40; Young, *Autobiography*, 319; Asbury, *Journal*, III, 396.
37 *Minutes*, I, 227; *Journals of the Ohio Conference*, 109-110. See, also, Redford, *Methodism in Kentucky*, II, 245.
38 *Journals of the Ohio Conference*, 104-105.
39 Redford, *Methodism in Kentucky*, II, 283.
40 Young, *Autobiography*, 309.
41 Finley, *Autobiography*, 250.
42 Paine, *William McKendree*, 241.
43 *Minutes*, I, 229, 245.

marked decrease may be attributed to several reasons, among the chief of which was war, which called many into army ranks and slackened the moral sense of others. Concerning this Cartwright stated: "This year [1812-1813] there was a considerable decrease in membership in the Methodist Episcopal Church, owing chiefly to the war with England; and we felt the sad effects of the war throughout the West."[44] A great many converts who professed following the earth disturbances were not at all permanent and in due time "returned to their evil habits."[45] As late as 1814 Asbury recorded, "There is distress everywhere—in the church and abroad in the United States."[46] A scarcity of preachers also may partially account for this diminution in the church rolls. The register of the ministry did not increase commensurately with the ever-widening circuits; consequently, there were extensive areas which no preacher served and which had no church contacts.

The damage and suffering from the war extended over the entire country. The rigorous blockade along the entire seaboard caused an extreme inflation in prices. At Charleston flour rose to nineteen dollars a barrel and to seventeen dollars at Boston. Tea, coffee, butter, molasses, and sugar were beyond the poor man's reach,[47] while staple products like wheat, flour, tobacco, and cotton had little or no market during the war.[48] These high prices did not restrict themselves to the coastal states; inland districts were affected, and there commodities reached exorbitant prices. The cost of living soared, and, in face of all the practices of frugality, incomes could not be stretched to furnish even the immediate necessities. The expectation of eighty dollars annually was fostered by the highest hopes, for collections were always poor. Even if they were good it is difficult to understand how eighty dollars would purchase rations for a year when pitted

---

44 Cartwright, *Autobiography*, 133.
45 Finley, *Autobiography*, 258.
46 Asbury, *Journal*, III, 433-434.
47 McMaster, *History of the United States*, IV, 217, 221, 222. See Channing, *History of the United States*, IV, 538-539.
48 K. C. Babcock, *The Rise of American Nationality* (New York, 1906), 188-189. After peace was signed there was a sudden reversal of prices, sugar was cut in half, and flour rose fifty per cent. See Henry Adams, *History of the United States during the Administrations of Jefferson and Madison* (9 vols., New York, 1889-1891), IX, 61. A valuable table giving current prices in cities from Boston to New Orleans may be found in *Niles Register*, V (1814), 41.

against salt that sold for five dollars a bushel and tea at four dollars a pound. For even Bishop Asbury there was little appropriation; at one time there were nine annual conferences each paying the Bishop nine dollars.[49] Many families were on the verge of absolute distress.[50]

McKendree and Asbury were present at both the Ohio and Tennessee conferences of 1813.[51] Concerning the slackened religious consciousness which continued to prevail, Asbury wrote: "The families in the neighborhood have not been unvisited; if in the midst of such terrors the people will not forsake the racecourse, why should the people of God neglect to frequent these meetings?"[52] The report on membership showed a noticeable decrease. A committee was appointed to prepare materials for the *History of Methodism* and the *American Methodist Magazine*. This organized literary effort must have failed as no other reference is made to such an endeavor.[53] At the Tennessee Conference considerable discussion was given to the question of slavery. Appointment of presiding elders remained identical with the 1813 placements. James Axley was kept on the Holston District, Learner Blackman at Nashville, and James Gwinn on the Cumberland.[54] Few names are outstanding among the appointments of the Tennessee Conference. The second generation was not of the same mettle as the first; the leaders of the Asbury and McKendree period had few equals in 1812-1824.

When the governmental body met again in Ohio, on September 8, 1814, McKendree was unable to be present. He had been thrown from his horse and was severely injured in his hip and ribs.[55] For that reason John Sale presided over the conference; McKendree, however, was improved sufficiently to attend the Tennessee meeting which convened during the latter part of September.[56] "Poor Bishops—sick, lame and in poverty."[57] These two venerable men had given of their best; Asbury

---

49 McFerrin, *Methodism in Tennessee*, II, 288.
50 Jones, *Methodism in Mississippi*, I, 379.
51 Redford, *Methodism in Kentucky*, II, 285-287; McFerrin, *Methodism in Tennessee*, II, 307-309.
52 Asbury, *Journal*, II, 423.
53 *Journals of the Ohio Conference*, 113.
54 *Minutes*, I, 230.
55 Asbury, *Journal*, III, 433; Paine, *William McKendree*, 252.
56 *Journals of the Ohio Conference*, 121.
57 Asbury, *Journal*, III, 435.

at the end of life, and McKendree the complete disciple who was yet in his prime. The church had been their bride, for it was the accepted convictions of both that only in a celibate life could they promote the best interests of the church. The scanty means of support and the vast field of pastoral labor induced them to remain unmarried. With the passing of years, however, it was proved that celibacy could not be expected of the clergy, and in due time Asbury and McKendree became reconciled to the fact that it was better for Methodist preachers to marry. To this Tennessee meeting Asbury brought ten dollars for every traveling preacher's child or children.[58] This money the senior bishop had begged from door to door in the older and wealthier communities in the East. In the old worn journal, which contained Asbury's thoughts and acts, he has written of this conference: "We closed our labors in peace and love. The families have been kind to us, but we were much crowded. We have lost members from the society, and gained, perhaps, one preacher in the itineracy in two years."[59] Even though the western conferences had experienced a loss for three years, Methodism had made a perceptible progress since it had crossed the mountains. Of this growth Asbury wrote, "One thing I remark—our Conferences are out of their infancy; their rulers can now be called from amongst ourselves."[60] Among these eminent leaders were William Adams,[61] Leroy Cole,[62] William Dixon,[63] Thomas L. Douglass,[64] Learner Blackman,[65] James Quinn, [66] James Axley,[67] and Peter Cartwright.[68]

---

[58] Cartwright, *Autobiography*, 140.
[59] Asbury, *Journal*, III, 436 He believed the strict Methodist discipline was partly responsible.
[60] *Ibid.*, III, 434.
[61] M. P. Gaddis, *Last Words and Old-Time Memories* (Cincinnati, 1880)', 11; Redford, *Methodism in Kentucky*, II, 304-311.
[62] *Ibid.*, II, 311-315.
[63] *Ibid.*, II, 318-320; McFerrin, *Methodism in Tennessee*, II, 339-342; Gaddis, *Old-Time Memories*, 10.
[64] McFerrin, *Methodism in Tennessee*, II, 346-376.
[65] Finley, *Sketches*, ch. xiv.
[66] Stevens, *History of Methodism*, 394-395, 473-474.
[67] Finley, *Sketches*, ch. xvi; Stevens, *History of Methodism*, 482-483.
[68] See Cartwright, *Autobiography* and Cartwright, *Fifty Years As a Presiding Elder;* also, Stevens, *History of Methodism*, 483-486; Milburn, *Ten Years of Preacher-Life*, 38-46, gives an excellent sketch of Cartwright. For Years the name of Cartwright stood out chief among servants, his duties were important. An omission of his name or activity from the history of this period is a grievous error.

The devastating influences of war had not been able to wipe out entirely all the social and religious activities of western life. The revivals had not been discarded by any means; many portions of the West were again scenes of interest in the camp meeting with its vociferous preacher. At Ebenezer in Wilson County, Tennessee, a camp meeting was conducted where 182 professed Christianity. In another meeting near Murfreesboro 330 professed and from that number 202 joined the church.[69] Notwithstanding these gains the minutes of the Tennessee Conference show 1815 to have been another year of loss in membership.[70]

The whole blame for losses in church membership cannot be laid, however, to the war. It must be remembered that new lands in the West had just been opened up, and the population began to pour into this section. For the past quarter of a century there had been a continuous movement westward, but the movement was now generally quickened; "dull times, the coast blockade, the taxes, and the disorders of the currency so accelerated it that in the winter of 1814 the exodus from the seaboard states became alarming."[71] Concerning the heavy loss which the Holston District bore, McAnally wrote:

> It will be recollected that early in the year peace had been proclaimed between the United States and England; and soon after large tracts of country were opened in the West and Southwest for occupancy, and to these hundreds of persons emigrated from the bounds of the Holston District, among whom were many Methodists, a fact that may, at least in part, account for the decreases in membership, notwithstanding some extensive revivals were experienced.[72]

In the fall of 1815 Asbury again traveled to the Ohio Conference. He was fast failing in health and had already surrendered all business matters to McKendree; only at a request of the conference did he preach a memorial sermon for Dr. Coke,[73] who had been found dead in his cabin when *en route* to Ceylon

---
[69] McFerrin, *Methodism in Tennessee*, II, 359, 361.
[70] *Minutes*, I, 260, 282.
[71] McMaster, *History of the United States*, IV, 383. For a rather thorough account of the rush westward see *ibid.*, IV, 381-387.
[72] McAnally, *Life and Times of Patton*, 149.
[73] Tipple, *Francis Asbury*, 289-290.

as a missionary in 1813.[74] From Ohio Asbury went to attend the Tennessee Conference which convened in Wilson County, Tennessee. His infirmities which were multiplying made the grand old man realize that his strength was gone. His diary for March 20-22 reads: "My eyes fail. I will resign the stations to Bishop McKendree—I will take away my feet. It is my fifty-fifth year of ministry, and forty-fifth year of labor in America. My mind enjoys great peace and consolation."[75] This was Asbury's last conference. For almost half of a century he had been untiring in his active ministry in America. Fresh in the vigor of youth he preached his first sermon in the new world at Philadelphia in 1771; as a worn-out old man he preached his last in Richmond.[76] The scope of his travel and labor is without equal. It has been estimated that Asbury preached from fifteen thousand to eighteen thousand sermons, presided at over two hundred conferences, ordained four thousand preachers, and traveled from 200,000 to 300,000 miles through American wildernesses.[77]

With his passing the Methodist Church was freed from many restrictions and prejudices which were essentially peculiar to the old bishop. A second day of independence began with the relaxation of Asbury's dominant rule.[78] The influence of Wesley had already moderated, and now again the old regime gave place to the new.

---

[74] Drew, *Life of Thomas Coke*, 350-369. See account of his death in the *Minutes*, I, 266-268.
[75] Asbury, *Journal*, III, 468. See Tipple, *Francis Asbury*, 291; Luccock, *The Story of Methodism*, 249-250; Cartwright, *Autobiography*, 152.
[76] Smith, *Francis Asbury*, 296-297; C. H. Prather, "Francis Asbury, Apostle," *Meth. Rev.* (Nashville, 1916), LXV, 323-333; J. O. Andrews, "Bishop Asbury," *Meth. Rev.* (Nashville, 1859), XIII, 1-11.
[77] H. K. Carroll, *Francis Asbury in the Making of American Methodism* (New York, 1923), 235.
[78] An excellent discussion of Asbury's use of power is found in Bacon, *History of American Christianity*, 200-201.

CHAPTER V

EDUCATIONAL EFFORTS AND ACHIEVEMENTS

The religious organizations in the early period of American history clearly felt that an educated ministry was an essential part of a successful church. In New England nineteen out of forty ministers of the first generation were college graduates, while the second generation furnished an even larger number of academically trained clergymen. In later years, at least by the middle of the eighteenth century, the standards were lowered in some degree. A proof of the intense desire for a college trained ministry may be found in the establishment of Harvard, Yale, and other colleges, the chief purpose of which was to train men for the work of the church. It is true that the immediate need for more ministers than the colleges were able to supply brought about a system of private instruction by individual pastors, who in many instances had been trained in the colleges. As a general rule, however, the Dutch, Anglican, Congregational, and Presbyterian churches recognized as essential a carefully trained ministry.[1]

With the Methodists the situation was strikingly different. Biographies, papers, letters, and other records show that the Methodist preachers were poorly educated in spite of the fact that Whitefield, the two Wesleys,[2] and Coke were university bred men. All four of these men were university graduates, and although Francis Asbury was not college trained, he was a student by his own will. John Wesley's enthusiasm was not weakened by his change of continents; it was with great feeling that he hotly exclaimed, "The Methodist are poor, but there is no need they should be ignorant."[3] He knew that the permanence of his work depended largely upon education. Dr. Coke was

---

[1] For this as well as several of the following paragraphs, I have drawn heavily upon the worthwhile study by Duvall, *The Methodist Church and Education.* For other sources on Methodist education see Cummings, *Early Schools of Methodism;* Hazel Mileham, *History of Higher Education of the Methodist Church in the United States from 1820-1844* (M. A. thesis, University of Chicago, 1926); L. M. Spivey, *Methodist Education in America Prior to 1820* (M. A. thesis, University of Chicago, 1922).
[2] As early as 1748 Wesley had opened his Kingswood (England) school. See sketch in Cummings, *Early Schools of Methodism,* 9-19. The part taken by Wesley in early Methodist philanthropy is traced in C. M. Woodward, *Philanthropic Aspects of Early Methodism* (B. D. thesis, University of Chicago, 1917).
[3] Quoted by Jarrell, *Methodism on the March,* 36.

EDUCATIONAL EFFORTS 63

sent to America to support the intellectual standard and to furnish material for a worthwhile successor. Dr. Coke, however, was able to exert little influence upon education in America.[4] His single effort was the unfortunate attempt to found and promote Cokesbury College, the name itself seemed to confess the personal vanities of both Coke and Asbury, and for it Wesley rebuked them severely.[5] Bangs stated that Asbury was to a certain degree prejudiced against a trained ministry.[6] Asbury's *Journal,* however, shows that not only was he interested in his own education,[7] but that he also gave much aid to educational enterprises.[8] Early in his ministry he nurtured the idea of establishing a boarding school, and by 1790 he was collecting subscriptions for the erection of such a school to be situated at Bethel, in Jessamine County, Kentucky. Almost five years (1794) passed before the project was completed on one hundred acres of remote land on the cliffs of the Kentucky River.[9] A number of students enrolled for academic training, but for many reasons the school declined, and in turn it was used for a common and then a neighborhood school. Little of definite history has been left concerning this undertaking. Inadequate support, unsettled conditions in the West, Indian raids, inaccessibility of the location, heavy tax on preacher's income—all contributed to the general debilitation of Bethel, and led to its final abandonment as a church school.[10]

Nevertheless, Asbury's vision was not to be ignored. His extensive travels brought before him the evidences of widespread ignorance; and, after the burning of Cokesbury, he renewed his

---

[4] Bishop J. O. Andrews said of Coke: "With all his acknowledged ability, zeal and piety, he did not understand the genius of American people." "Bishop McKendree," *Meth. Rev.* (Nashville, 1859), XIII, 164.

[5] J. A. Faulkner, *The Methodists* (New York, 1903), 203-204.

[6] Bangs, *History of the Methodist Church,* II, 413-414.

[7] One of the twenty-eight pages of the index to the 1852 edition of Asbury's *Journal* contains Asbury's reading list.

[8] See his *Journal,* I, 191, 206; II, 63, 76, 85, 175. As early as 1780 Asbury planned to establish an academy in America. *Journal,* I, 377. The fact that Asbury had established by the date of his death (1816) one or more schools in every conference in America caused one historian to honor him with the title of the first "Commissioner of Education of the United States." Jarrell, *Methodism on the March,* 122.

[9] Asbury, *Journal,* II, 85, 148, 193, 260, 294, 473.

[10] Finley, *Sketches,* 42-43. It is of interest to note that in the erection of Engineering Hall on the Vanderbilt University campus a corner stone taken from the ruins of Bethel Academy was placed in the structure. For a picture of this stone see E. S. Tipple, *The Heart of Asbury's Journal* (Cincinnati, 1904), 579.

district schools in various sections of the country.¹¹

The Methodist's early lack of interest in education may easily and satisfactorily be explained. When Asbury came to America, he found thousands of the inhabitants living outside of any church, because there were no preachers to minister to them. What was the most effective way of supplying these people with preachers? The decision came thoughtfully and yet promptly. They should be recruited from the ranks.¹² Wherever Asbury or his traveling companion found a young man¹³ with talent interested in the ministry, this one was engaged in a subordinate work until he gave evidence of fitness for additional responsibility. It was a great temptation to call into service any robust man of religious sincerity and good judgment even though he was lacking in academic training.¹⁴ Striking examples are found in the *Journal of the Western Conference* that such men were enlisted into the service as "William Pattison, who has travilled 3 months on the Miami Circuit. A man of little education and small abilities, but is said to be pious, zealous, and useful, and came well recommended." Also "Abraham Amos, who has been in profession of religion two and a half years, of small gifts, and eliterate; but was useful and much esteemed in his neighborhood." The conference allowed to remain on trial "Ralph Lotspiech, a man some what peculiar, but is thought to improve, and amend."¹⁵ By reading at intervals the recruit was able to acquire knowledge enough to make himself a power for good among the people.

During these formative years of Western Methodism the frontier spokesman had what the young nation needed, the will to do and the soul to dare. No belief could be more in error than the somewhat current one that the real leaders of the church desired an uneducated clergy. They were afraid, however, of the experiment of education.¹⁶ The theology was simple, easy to state and easy to apply, and the church elders feared that the

---

11 Faulkner, *The Methodists*, 207.
12 Cartwright, *Autobiography*, 4; Cleveland, *The Great Revival*, 50; Sellers, *Lorenzo Dow*, 93.
13 A few of the characteristics desired in a young preacher may be learned from a "Letter to a Junior Preacher," *Meth. Mag.*, VII (1824), 111-114.
14 Mode, *Frontier Spirit*, 63-64.
15 *Journal of the Western Conference*, 84, 85.
16 See an interesting comment recorded in the *Minutes of the Indiana Conference*, 1832-1844 regarding a seminary educated ministry. "We are well aware that when a conference seminary is named, some of our people suppose we are about

EDUCATIONAL EFFORTS

frigidity of a formal education might chill the ardor and enthusiasm of the native sons. "In a word, they feared, and they feared rightly a professional clergy. And a professional clergy then, now and always is a hireling clergy."[17]

Because of the vast number of illiterates in the west, for whom Methodism had an especial appeal, the authorities thought nothing to be a more sinful waste of time than preparation for a trained ministry. Some frontier itinerants even thought that book learning would be a hindrance to their success. "Many preachers," as Cartwright phrased it, "murdered the King's English at every lick";[18] yet, this lack of education did not disqualify them for the task which was theirs. The educated preaching groups were misfits among the plain frontier folk and in the rugged environment. They were likened to "lettuce growing under the shade of a peach tree, or like a gosling that had got the straddles by wading in the dew."[19] Sharp repartee, abundant sympathy, and earnestness in behavior were more necessary for the missionary type than all the polished manners learned in college halls.[20] The choice made by the church was "not between an illiterate and learned ministry; but between an illiterate and no ministry at all."[21] Few will doubt that it was better to have such men preach than none at all. This concensus of Methodist opinion brought forth an early editorial:

> Let those happy thousands answer the question who have heard the soul cheering voice of these men in the wilderness. They followed them, or rather went with them to dreary canebreaks, and lonely groves; where instead of the sound of the 'church-going bell' was heard the savage war-whoop, and the dampening voice of ruinous beasts. Let those, we say, judge of these preachers, and their usefulness, who have been favored with their society, and their pious labors, when forted among savages, in the wilderness, when first cabbined on the newly

---

to establish a manufactory in which preachers are to be made. But nothing is farther from our views, for we are fully aware of Mr. Bernge's opinion, when comparing ministers to pens, observes that although the Seminaries have been trying to make pens for some hundreds of years, they will not write until God nibs them." Sweet, *Circuit Rider Days in Indiana*, 101.

17 E. S. Tipple, "Methodism and Theological Education," *Christian Advocate*, CI (1926), 1157.
18 Cartwright, *Autobiography*, 6; Sellers, *Lorenzo Dow*, 93.
19 Cartwright, *Autobiography*, 80.
20 Channing, *History of the United States*, V, 232.
21 "Learned Ministers," *Holston Messenger*, III (1828), 209.

opened farms, and who have accompanied them through the various incidents of changing fortunes, until our once howling wilderness is converted into fruitful fields, and cultivated gardens.[22]

A comparison of the Methodist expansion with that of other churches will no doubt prove the wisdom of the circuit plan. The unlettered preacher of the Methodist Church who came often certainly was a more potent and more worthwhile factor in the evangelizing of the West than the learned, college trained ministry of some of the other sects who seldom visited the frontier people.[23] All denominations were faced with the paucity of numbers in their ranks, and a preacher could not be spared from the center of population. A circuit system was very effectively operated by the Methodists and proved to be the key to their success.

The passing of years, however, lessened the urgency for a hastily prepared ministry, and the Methodist mind began to give consideration to educational enterprises. In fact the ascendancy of other denominations in colleges and schools pressed the Methodist Church to take measures, since it was being left behind in this field. A list of early colleges that yet exist bears testimony to the activity of the state governments or of various denominations in the early Northwest: Ohio University (State, 1803), Miami (State, 1809), Kenyon (Protestant Episcopal, 1826), McKendree (Methodist, 1828), Oberlin (State, 1833), and Knox (non-sectarian, 1837). The Methodist attitude toward the promotion of education changed for several reasons—contact with other sects, interdenominational discussions on theology, increasing wealth of the church, and growth of the press and its far-reaching influence.

The most interesting educational undertaking of the Methodists, and also the most notable failure, was Cokesbury College near Baltimore,[24] whose opening, December 6-10, 1787, was marked by an ominous sermon by Bishop Asbury from the fore-

---

22 *Idem.*
23 Presbyterians, for example. See Rusk, *Literature of the Frontier*, I, 64.
24 For Coke's description after visiting Cokesbury see Drew, *Life of Thomas Coke*, 120; J. L. Seaton, "Methodism and Education," *Christian Advocate*, CI (1926), 1153.

boding text, "O, thou Man of God, there is death in the pot."[25] The rules which Asbury and Coke made for controlling the students were stringent. Early rising and early retiring were required; no provision was made for play or gardening; walking and riding were considered as recreation. The students were denied even the luxury of feather beds as they were considered unhealthful.[26] The building was destroyed by fire on December 4, 1795. Later, after the school was revived in the form of Washington College, fire took its toll the second time (1796),[27] and, as a result, Methodist educational progress was checked for several years.[28]

The *Discipline* of 1784 directed the preachers to study for five hours a day and to preach at intervals on the subject of education.[29] Thirty-two years were allowed to elapse before further consideration was given to this phase of church effort. At this time a new interest was expressed in the minutes, as follows:

> We perceive a manifest defect among us . . . in regard to ministerial education. Although a collegiate education is not . . . deemed essential to a gospel ministry, yet it appears absolutely necessary . . . that a workman . . . who would be useful . . . should add an ardent desire for useful knowledge. He should strive by every science which . . . will enable him to understand and illustrate the sacred Scripture . . . . The manifest influence of some . . . [who are] stripping the Church of some of its brightest ornaments, not only exposes her nakedness, but calls loudly for the prompt and vigorous interference of the General Conference.[30]

The general church body conceived great ideas but went little beyond the conception, for after some elaborate rules were

---
25 Asbury, *Journal*, II, 22.
26 "Education in the Methodist Episcopal Church, South," *Meth. Rev.* (Nashville, 1859), XIII, 13.
27 W. Hamilton, "Early Methodism in Maryland, Especially in Baltimore," *Meth. Rev.* (New York, 1856), XXXVIII, 445-447. Cartwright (*Fifty Years As A Presiding Elder*, 213) said of the burning of Cokesbury: "God set it on fire and burned it up. They said it was a negro, but I believe the Lord did it, for they got into a quarrel over it and He ended it in that way by fire." Such a burden was this educational effort to Asbury that he wrote: "Would any man give me 10,000 pounds a year to do and suffer what I have done for that house [Cokesbury], I would not do it." *Journal*, II, 287. The college was at all times in financial straits. Asbury, *Journal*, II, 116, 138, 155, 209.
28 Faulkner, *The Methodists*, 203-204, 207.
29 Duvall, *The Methodist Church and Education*, 42.
30 *Journals of the General Conference*, I, 149.

passed in 1796 to govern schools and colleges then unorganized, no action was taken for the building of such schools before 1820. By this date plans long dormant sprang into activity, and within a period of five years attention was directed to the education of both clergy and the laity. At the General Conference of 1820 a committee was appointed "to inquire into the expediency of digesting and recommending the outline of a plan for the institution of schools." And in that year it was recommended to all the annual conferences to establish, as soon as practicable, literary institutions, under their own control in such a way and manner as they might think proper. Four years later the General Conference approved this resolution[31] and thereby the Church was committed to an active educational program.[32] In spite of this definite plan, progress was so slow that Nathan Bangs, one of the most ardent advocates of the resolution said:

> That opposition should be manifested to these efforts to raise the standard of education by any of the disciples of the illustrious Wesley, whose profound learning added so much splendor to his character as an evangelical minister, may seem strange to some. This, however, was the fact; and their unreasonable opposition exemplified in a variety of ways, tended not a little to paralyze for a season, the efforts of those who had enlisted in this cause; while the apathy of others retarded its progress and made its final success somewhat uncertain.[33]

Augusta, the first Methodist college in Kentucky, was opened in 1822. Nevertheless, its background extended as far as 1798 when the legislators of Kentucky deeded to the citizens of Bracken County six thousand acres of land on which was to be established Bracken Academy at Augusta on the Ohio River. This land was held by the trustees until the price had advanced considerably. The fund from its sale went to Bracken Academy and there remained until 1822 when it was transferred to Augusta College.[34] In 1821 the Ohio Conference appointed a committee to meet with the Kentucky Conference in an effort to "unite in

---

31 *Ibid.*, I, 149, 186, 208, 295. The "Report of the Committee on Education" for the General Conference of 1824 is contained in *Meth. Mag.*, VII (1824), 276-277.
32 McTyeire, *History of Methodism*, 567; "Education in the Methodist Episcopal Church, South," *Meth. Rev.* (Nashville, 1859), XIII, 14-15.
33 Bangs, *History of the Methodist Church*, III, 107.
34 Mileham, *Higher Education of the Methodist Church*, 12.

the establishment of a college under their joint patronage."[35] The Kentucky Conference was thoroughly in favor of the movement. The two commissioners appointed by each conference visited Augusta, Kentucky, on December 15, 1821, and there held a conference with the trustees of Bracken Academy. They made known their plan to found a college at Augusta, "provided a little assistance could be obtained from the trustees of the Academy and citizens in building a college edifice and giving the institution a start until the conferences could sufficiently command their resources, when they would amply endow the same as an institution worthy the people for whose benefit they were laboring."[36] This appeal fell upon such receptive ears that the trustees of Bracken Academy agreed to give the proceeds of the fund and all of the principal above ten thousand dollars. The college was chartered by the Kentucky legislature on December 7, 1822. John P. Finley was its first president. At the time of its incorporation it was the only Methodist college possessing the right to confer degrees.[37]

Practically every stationed preacher of all sects conducted an elementary school in connection with his church duties. By this means an additional service was rendered to the community and an additional income was secured for the preacher and his family.[38] The schoolhouse was the ordinary log structure in which tousled headed children pored over Dilsworth's *Speller* or thumbed the leaves of a *New Testament*. Geography and arithmetic they learned by rote, and writing proved so difficult that few ever went beyond "capitals" and large joining hand.[39]

The Presbyterians were the pioneers in education in Tennessee.[40] Four ministers[41] of this faith have written their names

---
35 The report of the Kentucky Conference is in Redford, *Methodism in Kentucky*, II, 98-99.
36 From an extract of a communication by James B. Finley, to whom chief honor must go for the establishment of Augusta. See Redford, *Methodism in Kentucky*, II, 99-100.
37 *Ibid.*, II, 100.
38 McAnally, *Life and Times of Patton*, 169-172; McAnally concedes to the Presbyterians the early supremacy of education in Tennessee.
39 Mileham, *Higher Education in the Methodist Church*, 13-14. For a description of early educational conditions in Kentucky see Perrin, *History of Kentucky*, 220-221. Early school life in Tennessee is described in W. T. Hale and D. L. Merritt, *A History of Tennessee and Tennesseans* (8 vols., Chicago, 1913), II, ch. xxv.
40 For the first school in Cumberland see B. W. McDonnold, *History of the Cumberland Presbyterian Church* (Nashville, 1899), 5-16.
41 Messrs. Doak, Craighead, Anderson, and Coffin.

indelibly into the history of Tennessee schools by the organization of four colleges,[42] which after many changes exist today. The membership of the Presbyterian Church had been drawn from the Scotch-Irish who possessed a passionate love for learning and religion.

Little is known of the early work of the Methodist Church in Tennessee education. State histories have given such matters little attention, no Tennessee Conference records of any session before 1872 remain,[43] and no report of the Conference Board of Education is to be found earlier than this date. The scattering commentaries tell us that this part of the work of the conference was negative.[44] McFerrin stated that as late as 1812, when the Tennessee Conference was organized, there was "no committee on education because there were no schools, and no thought of establishing any at that period."[45]

The year 1820 marked a growing interest in education, not only in the General Conference but also in the Tennessee Annual Conference.[46] Since there was no Committee on Education all matters were referred to the Committee on Missions which brought in the following report:

> Resolved: 1. That a committee be appointed by this Conference to confer with the trustees of Bethel Academy, at Nicholasville, Jessamine County, Kentucky.[47]
>
> 2. That the committee be instructed to meet as soon as possible and enter into such measures as may seem best in their judgment to employ a teacher as soon as the present session concludes.
>
> 3. That the committee have power to enter into such measures as they may deem most expedient for raising such sums of money as may be necessary, and that they communicate such plan to the presiding elders of the Kentucky Conference, whose duty it shall be to put such plan or plans into operation.

---

[42] Washington, Greeneville, East Tennessee, and Southwestern Theological Seminary.
[43] Earlier records were destroyed when the Methodist Publishing House, in Nashville, was burned in May, 1872.
[44] A brief summary of education of the Methodist and Presbyterian churches in Tennessee is contained in R. G. Peoples, "Secondary Education in the Tennessee Conference," *Tenn. Conf. Jour.*, 1912, pp. 133-138.
[45] McFerrin, *Methodism in Tennessee*, II, 312.
[46] W. F. Tillett, "Methodism and Higher Education in the Tennessee Conference," *Tenn. Conf. Jour.* 1912, pp. 139-155. This is primarily devoted to the years beyond the scope of this study.
[47] At that time under control of Jessamine County.

EDUCATIONAL EFFORTS

4. That the presiding elders of the Tennessee Annual Conference be instructed to make inquiry with respect to the most eligible site for erecting a seminary, and of the most probable means of raising money for its establishment, as also to receive any donations that may be given, conditionally or otherwise, for the purpose, and report to the next Annual Conference.[48]

This was undoubtedly the first effort to build an institution of learning in the Tennessee Conference. The following year (1821) the conference again considered the question of building a seminary. On the motion of Robert Paine, the conference appointed a committee of three to take charge of the matter, one of whom should correspond with the Mississippi Conference and invite them to co-operate in the establishment of such an institution. In case they failed to unite, the work was to be carried on by selecting a site within the conference, raising money, erecting buildings, and employing teachers, and reporting to the annual conference at the next meeting. Nothing materialized from these elaborate plans for several years. As late as 1824 there was not within the bounds of the Tennessee Conference, according to McAnally, "a single school of high grade under their control or over which they could exercise any important influence."[49] On the other hand, the Presbyterians had control of every important educational institution in that territory; this insured for them a wonderful power and influence in fashioning the thought of the youth.[50]

So it was that the Methodist Church awakened suddenly to the realization that the erection of new institutions of learning, under the immediate control of the church, was a necessity. None of the schools founded between 1784 and 1819 had remained permanent[51] in spite of the interest and financial aid from bishops and congregations. These early schools had been located as a rule in remote places, away from towns, in order to protect the students from temptation.[52] Consequently, the very

---
48 Report in McFerrin, *Methodism in Tennessee*, III, 184-185.
49 McAnally, *Life and Times of Patton*, 169.
50 Edwin Paschall, *Old Times or Tennessee History for Tennessee Boys and Girls* (Nashville, 1869), 291-292.
51 Cummings, *Early Schools of Methodism*, 424, 426.
52 McTyeire, *History of Methodism*, 449.

location had in a measure defeated the continuance of such schools. They were outside of easy communication and accessibility to the more thickly populated sections. But success in time followed the failures and discouragements of the first thirty-five years. The *Holston Messenger* of 1828[53] claimed that one thousand students were enrolled in Methodist institutions of learning in America. Following the founding of Augusta College further educational endeavors introduced to Western Methodism such institutions as La Grange College (1830), La Grange, Alabama; Wesleyan Female College (1836), Macon, Georgia; Emory College (1836), Oxford, Georgia; Emory and Henry College (1838), Emory, Virginia; Athens College (1843), Athens, Alabama; and a host of lesser ones.[54]

Various reasons may be assigned for the failure of practically every educational effort made by the church before 1825. Perhaps the outstanding reason was a financial one—early Methodist people belonged to the poorer class and were unable to make substantial contributions. Asbury wrote: "The poverty of the people and the general scarcity of money is the great source of our difficulty.... We have the poor, but they have no money, and the rich we do not care to ask."[55]

Organized effort within the Methodist Church for the establishment of Sunday schools was contemporary with the endeavor of instituting schools for higher education. The same dilatoriness accompanied this effort, with the result that nothing noteworthy was achieved before 1825. The plan of schools for religious training of the young, however, has been for the past century such a vital and interwoven part of the present system for religious growth that its beginnings must be examined regardless of their feebleness.

---

53 *Holston Messenger*, III (1828), 207.
54 Jarrell, *Methodism on the March*, 124; Cummings, *Early Schools of Methodism*, 427. The dates given for the founding of these schools vary in many sources.
55 Asbury, *Journal*, III, 63. The change in the attitude of some Methodist preachers toward education borders on the ludicrous. Cartwright who had once hurled anathemas against the "velvet-mouthed and downy D. D.'s" (Cartwright, *Autobiography*, 410) later accepted a doctor's degree. Cartwright, *Fifty Years As a Presiding Elder*, 215-216. So eager did the Western preachers become for the "hollow titles" that some wanted to make it a rule that as soon as a preacher graduated to elder's orders he would receive a D. D. degree. Brunson, *Western Pioneer*, I, 392-393. This matter progressed so far as to be made the work of a committee in the General Conference of 1832. *Journals of the General Conference*, I, 399. The report of the committee suffered "an indefinite postponement." *Ibid.*, I, 412.

The first institution deserving the name of a Sunday school began with Cardinal Borromeo (1538-1584), the eminent Archbishop of Milan, who devoted himself to the training of the neglected children of his city. Evidence indicates that the first Sunday school in the Protestant churches sprang up in Roxbury, Massachusetts, in 1658.[56] An idea similar to this one was brought to America in the fertile mind of John Wesley and was put into practice by catechizing on Sunday the children of his parish in Savannah, Georgia.[57] So eager was Wesley to interest the children that when the poor ones came without shoes, he immediately took off his own in order to make these children feel at ease.[58] Disregarding some isolated cases,[59] there was no general system of Sunday schools in England or America before the year 1784 when Robert Raikes began his school in Gloucester, where lived many people who were engaged in pen manufacturing. Raikes inquired of a gardener's wife the cause for the neglect of the children. Her rather indignant reply was, "Oh, sir! If you were here on a Sunday, you would pity them indeed: we cannot read our Bibles in peace for them."[60] This served to arouse Raikes to the necessity of educating the children of the poor. Immediately teachers were hired for the purpose of imparting to the children the rudiments of a common education. The children went to the teacher at ten o'clock each Sunday morning and remained until twelve. After an hour spent at home for lunch they returned again at one, and remained until five-thirty, the dismissal hour. Raikes brought much criticism upon himself with his school; he was accused of violating the Sabbath, and of invading the ranks of aristocracy by teaching the

---

56 J. D. McClintock, "The Sunday School in its Relation to the Church," *Meth. Rev.* (Nashville, 1857), XI, 516.

57 W. B. Stevens, *A History of Georgia from its Discovery by Europeans to the Adoption of the Present Constitution in* 1798 (2 vols., New York, 1847), I, 341.

58 Addie Wardle, *History of the Sunday School Movement in the Methodist Episcopal Church* (New York, 1918), 15; J. O. A. Clark, "Methodism—Modern Sunday Schools," *Meth. Rev.* (Nashville, 1884), VI, 624.

59 In Germantown, Pennsylvania, there was a Sunday school established in 1738 and operated regularly until 1744, and then sporadically for some time, eventually being discontinued altogether during the time of the Revolution. It was established by Christopher Sower, a German printer of that city, in the German Brethren sect. C. S. Driver, *The Effect of their Environment on the Social, Educational, and Religious Practices of the German Baptist Brethren* (M. A. thesis, Vanderbilt University, 1924), 128.

60 "Origin of Sunday Schools," *Meth. Mag.,* IX (1826), 151.

children of factory folk to read and write. A few people, however, saw the value of his labor[61] and appreciated his task.

To whom the credit belongs for establishing the first Sunday school in America is a much mooted point.[62] As early as 1778 John Wesley was exhorting the people "to engage in the work for conscience and not for lucre's sake."[63] By 1788 the work in Boston had reached considerable magnitude as is attested by the following account by John Wesley:

> Sunday, April 20, about three, I met between nine hundred and a thousand of the children belonging to our Sunday school. I never saw such a sight before; they were all exactly clean, as well as plain in their apparel; all were serious and well behaved .... what is best of all many of them truly fear God, and some rejoice in his salvation. These are a pattern for all the town. Their usual diversion is to visit the poor that are sick, to exhort, to comfort, and pray with them; frequently ten or more get together and sing by themselves; sometimes thirty or forty; and are so earnestly engaged, alternately singing, praying and crying, that they know not how to part.[64]

No sooner had Wesley heard of Raikes' plan than he issued his approval of it in the *Arminian Magazine*.[65] The first American *Discipline* (1784) contained a section from the English rules which urged all preachers to train and instruct the children of the parish in the ways of the Lord.[66] Francis Asbury immediately felt the responsibility of the charge, and by 1786 had organized a school in Hanover County, Virginia, at the house of Thomas Crenshaw.[67] In 1790 he was conducting such a school

---

61 For additional material on the background and early beginning of the Sunday school movement see "Memoir of Robert Raikes, Esq.," *Meth. Mag.*, XI (1828), 292-302. An account of Raikes' school from a letter written by Raikes may be found in the *Arminian Magazine*, 1785, pp. 41-43.
62 Wardle, *Sunday School Movement*, 15, gives the credit to Elliott. The supporters of Asbury's claim are probably greater in number. See Bangs, *History of the Methodist Church*, I, 309-310; Finley, *Autobiography*, 388-389; Duvall, *The Methodist Church and Education*, 25; "The Sunday School Union of the Methodist Episcopal Church," *Meth. Mag.*, XI (1828), 350; McClintock, "The Sunday School in its Relation to the Church," *Meth. Rev.* (Nashville, 1857), XI, 518.
63 *Journal* for Saturday, April 19, 1778, and Sunday, April 20, 1778. See, also, Jarrell, *Methodism on the March*, 202.
64 Quoted in "Sunday Schools," *Holston Messenger*, III (1828), 77.
65 "The Sunday School Union of the Methodist Episcopal Church," *Meth. Mag.*, XI (1828), 349.
66 Duvall, *The Methodist Church and Education*, 25.
67 Clark, "Methodism—Modern Sunday Schools," *Meth. Rev.* (Nashville, 1884), VI, 630-631.

EDUCATIONAL EFFORTS

in Charleston for both blacks and whites.[68] In that same year the Charleston Methodist Conference passed a rule for the instruction of the poor children, white and black, in Sunday schools. The *Minutes* read:

> Let us labor as the heart and soul of one man to establish Sunday schools in or near the place of public worship. Let persons be appointed by the bishops, elders, deacons or preachers to teach (gratis) all that will attend and have capacity to learn . . . . [69]

This is said to be the first account of church legislation on the subject, and thereby the first recognition of a Sunday school by an American church.[70] In the "Notes to the Discipline" (1796) the bishops urged "the people in the cities, towns and villages to establish Sunday Schools wherever practicable for the benefit of the children of the poor."[71]

It is quite obvious that the idea of the Sunday school was restricted to teaching poor children to read in order that they might learn the Scriptures and thereby be brought under the influence of the church. In the beginning the plan did not include children of pious members of the church, but the scope was steadily enlarged, until it soon included all children. Within the next twenty years the Sunday school movement was so extensive that unions for the promotion of Sunday school work were organized in New York (1816), Boston (1816), and Philadelphia (1817). The Philadelphia Union was reorganized in 1824, and later became the American Sunday School Union. The *Christian Advocate* gave hearty support by publishing in 1828 a series of "Letters on Sunday School Instruction."[72] After a year this was changed to more formal lessons, and the weekly "Bible Class Lessons" began to appear in the *Advocate*.[73]

---

68 Duvall, *The Methodist Church and Education*, 25.
69 Quoted in Wardle, *Sunday School Movement*, 52; A. A. Brown, "The Sunday School Movement—A Century of Development," *Christian Advocate*, CI (1926), 1155.
70 Clark, "Methodism—Modern Sunday Schools," *Meth. Rev.* (Nashville, 1884), VI, 630-631.
71 Quoted by McClintock, "The Sunday School in its Relations to the Church," *Meth. Rev.* (Nashville, 1857), XI, 518.
72 Brown, "The Sunday School Movement—A Century of Development," *Christian Advocate*, CI (1926), 1155.
73 "The Christian Advocate, 1826-1926," *Christian Advocate*, CI (1926), 1094.

The General Conference of 1824 went on record regarding the promotion of Sunday schools:

> Resolved, by the delegates of the Annual Conferences in General Conference assembled, 1. That, as far as practicable it shall be the duty of every preacher of a circuit or station to obtain the names of the children belonging to his congregation; to form them into classes for the purpose of giving them religious instruction, to instruct them regularly himself, as much as his duties will allow; to appoint a suitable leader for each class, who shall instruct them in his absence, and to leave his successor a correct account of each class thus formed with the name of its leader.[74]

By the close of the period of this study (1824) scarcely any Sunday school legislation had been passed. Modern Sunday schools belong to a later period. Methodism's lack of interest, or rather, effort, in educational endeavors account for its slowness in organizing schools for children. And yet in spite of this fact the Methodists led the other denominations in providing religious care and instruction for the young.[75] The part taken by children in some of the early revivals, no doubt, spurred the church leaders on the frontier to make a more adequate provision for them.

In 1820 there went to Nashville, Tennessee, a young man named Samuel Ament, a son of a prominent Methodist minister in Kentucky. His acquaintance was limited to the Hon. Felix Grundy and his wife. The latter was a devoted Presbyterian and had conceived a plan for educating poor children and for giving them religious instruction. Young Ament was asked to become one of the teachers of the newly organized school. So the earliest Sunday school in the city of Nashville, and probably in the state of Tennessee, met on the first Sunday in July, 1820, in a dilapidated little frame building in the rear of the present McKendree Church.[76] At the first meeting there were present Mrs. Grundy, Samuel Ament, Nathan Ewing, Mildred Moore, and fifteen children. The books used were Webster's *Spelling Book* and the

---

[74] *Journals of the General Conference*, I, 295.
[75] Bangs, *History of the Methodist Church*, I, 310.
[76] McFerrin, *Methodism in Tennessee*, III, 152-153. This is the only valuable account of Sunday schools in Tennessee or Kentucky prior to 1824 that I have yet located. See Clayton, *Davidson County, Tennessee*, 326.

EDUCATIONAL EFFORTS

New Testament. Regularly each Sunday morning at eight o'clock the school met. The program was very similar to that of today, being composed of singing, praying, and class study.[77]

The school had no sooner got under way than a protest burst forth. The organizers were accused of being Sabbath breakers, violators of the law, and disturbers of the peace. Strange to say, the churches were foremost in the opposition against the Sunday school. They rose up and declared that never would they countenance the organization. Winter came on and found the shabby building in no condition to protect the children from the weather. Permission was asked to remove the Sunday school to the basement of the Methodist church. This was refused and the school was abandoned for the winter. With the first sign of spring, Mrs. Grundy and Mrs. McGavock revived the school in the basement of an old house on the corner of Church and Front streets. The building had originally been used as a cabinet shop for the manufacture of furniture, but some years later had been improvised into pig sties. These were the best quarters obtainable for the Sunday school. The fight waged by the churches against the school did not cease. One Sunday morning during 1822 the eyes of citizens walking along Church Street were attracted to a large piece of pasteboard suspended from the door of the Methodist church on which were written these words: "No desecration of the holy Sabbath, by teaching on the Sabbath in this Church." Soon after this, however, the Rubicon was crossed. Rev. Thomas Maddin followed by a number of the leading citizens of Nashville came to the aid of the little Sunday school in the basement of the old furniture shop. Winter again was near, and these quarters would not serve. An effort was made to get into the churches and this time success crowned the attempt. In November, 1822, the churches opened their doors and invited the Sunday school. This school on Sunday had no particular affiliation with any church. Dr. Maddin claimed to have put into operation the first regularly organized Sunday school in Nashville. If this meant connection with a specific denomination, his contentions are cor-

---

77 McFerrin, *Methodism in Tennessee,* III, 153.

rect. In the winter of 1823 Isaac Paul, an apprentice boy, organized two Sunday schools in Nashville, one of which was peculiarly called "Elysian Grove."[78]

The turning point in the Sunday school history of the church came on April 2, 1827, with the formation of the Sunday School Union,[79] which according to article two of the constitution was

> to promote the formation, and to concentrate the efforts of Sabbath schools connected with the congregations of the Methodist Episcopal Church, and others that may become auxiliary: to aid in the instruction of the rising generation, particularly in the knowledge of the Holy Scriptures, and in the service and worship of God.[80]

Three years after the formation of the Union more than 2,400 schools and 158,000 scholars were reported throughout the whole of American Methodism.[81] The work had grown by leaps and bounds, because of the fact that the church had recognized the Sunday school in its legislation and "clearly incorporated it with the whole system of its ecclesiastical and pastoral work."[82]

If the Methodist Episcopal Church was neglectful of organized formal education, it did in some degree balance the scales by providing reading material and a means for the general circulation of books.[83] A "book room" was in Wesley's original plan; and by this method he hoped to reach the masses of the people. Five years after the organization of the church in America, a "Book Concern" was instituted in Philadelphia under the editorship of John Dickens.[84] The shop was opened at a

---

[78] *Ibid.*, III, 153-156.
[79] Wardle, *Sunday School Movement*, 61.
[80] The constitution is in *Meth. Mag.*, X (1827), 368. For first annual report see *ibid.*, XI (1828), 349-352.
[81] Luccock, *The Story of Methodism*, 455. "Sabbath Schools in the West," *Holston Messenger*, IV (1829), 27-29, states that in the Western states with a population of four million only twenty thousand children were receiving benefits from Sunday school instruction.
[82] McClintock, "The Sunday School in its Relation to the Church," *Meth. Rev.* (Nashville, 1857), XI, 514. It was not, however, until 1836 that the General Conference instructed preachers to form Sunday schools in their charges whenever it was practicable, and not until 1840 was it the preacher's duty to make a report to the quarterly conference on the number and state of Sunday schools. Jarrell, *Methodism on the March*, 205. See, also, A. B. Hart, *Slavery and Abolition* (New York, 1906), 12.
[83] Eddy, "Influence of Methodism upon the Civilization and Education of the West," *Meth. Rev.* (New York, 1857), XXXIX, 290-291.
[84] W. F. Whitlock, *The Story of the Book Concerns* (Concinnati, 1903), 13-20.

EDUCATIONAL EFFORTS

personal expense of 120 pounds to Dickens; and two years of operation under his able management revealed a successful concern.[85] Among the first books printed by the Book Concern was a translation by Wesley of Thomas a Kempis' *Imitation of Christ*. Other products of the press for the first year were the *Hymn Book, Discipline,* and *Arminian Magazine*.[86] This was the initial gesture of a magnificent undertaking, and occasionally these publications would reach the frontier people.[87] The lack of adequate postal service brought about the use of the traveling preacher as a means of circulation for such publications. Saddle bags bulged with books and pamphlets, which were carried to remote settlements and sold by the preacher at the close of the meeting or anywhere on the circuit.[88] The taste for reading had so rapidly increased that in the last four years of Dickens' editorship 114,000 copies of books had been circulated among sixty thousand Methodists in America.[89] The need was yet great in the West. Samuel Mills and Daniel Smith, having traveled the West in 1814 and 1815 on a missionary survey and for the distribution of religious literature, reported that they found approximately seventy-six thousand families between the Allegheny Mountains and the Mississippi River without a Bible. To answer this need, the American Bible Society was formed in 1816.[90] Closely allied with the Book Concern was the Tract Society, which was organized in New York in 1817 with the aim of co-operating in the circulation of cheap religious publications which came from the press of the Book Concern.[91]

---

85 "Publishers of the Christian Advocate, 1826-1926," *Christian Advocate*, CI (1926), 1108-1109; Luccock, *The Story of Methodism*, 368-369; W. F. Conner, "The Book Committee—What It Is and What It Does," *Christian Advocate*, CI (1926), 1180.

86 F. A. Archibald (ed.), *Methodism and Literature: A Series of Articles from Several Writers on the Literary Enterprises and Achievements of the Methodist Episcopal Church* (New York, 1883), 21. From his own pen, Wesley gave to the press 371 publications, two-thirds of which sold for less than a shilling and one-fourth of which sold for a penny. See *Meth. Rev.* (New York, 1912), XCIV, 274-275; Robert Emory, *The Life of Rev. John Emory* (New York, 1841), 235-236.

87 For literature in the West see McMaster, *History of the United States*, V, 272-274, and note on 274; Cartwright, *Autobiography*, 178, 179.

88 D. G. Downey, "The Fountain of Books," *Christian Advocate*, CI (1926), 1182.

89 "Publishers of the Christian Advocate, 1826-1926," *Christian Advocate*, CI (1926), 1109.

90 McMaster, *History of the United States*, IV, 554.

91 McTyeire, *History of Methodism*, 563.

The Book Concern continued to expand,[92] and in the year 1820 the General Conference decided that a branch should be organized and located at Cincinnati.[93] This center was to supply the West with the books which were wagoned and shipped to Cincinnati by way of Philadelphia.[94] Martin Ruter was placed in charge of the Cincinnati "book room." From this office the westerners could also secure the several magazines now published under the patronage of the church. The publication of the *Methodist Magazine* was begun in 1818, and it was issued each month until 1828 when its title was changed to the *Methodist Magazine and Quarterly Review*. This periodical filled a great gap in frontier society—ten thousand subscribers the first year[95] is the most convincing evidence. The magazine flourished and was the forerunner of the *Methodist Review*. Encouraged by the success of the *Methodist Magazine,* another periodical appeared in 1823, *The Zion Herald,* a weekly magazine, published in Boston;[96] this, however, endured the financial strain for barely five years. It was not until September 9, 1826, that the really vital organ of the whole church was begun. *The Christian Advocate*[97] came from the press with five thousand copies, which were soon exhausted. Before it was a year old its subscription list counted fifteen thousand subscribers. Two ephemeral Western publications, *The Holston Conference Messenger* and the *Augusta Herald* (Kentucky), were soon merged with the *Christian Advocate*.[98]

---

[92] Four years later the assets of the book concern were $270,002.28 with $48,542.50 in liabilities. For statement see Emory, *Life of John Emory,* 241.
[93] *Journals of the General Conference,* I, 225; Whitlock, *The Book Concerns,* 39-40; Archibald, *Methodism and Literature,* 23-24.
[94] The business had been moved from Philadelphia to New York in 1808. Whitlock, *The Book Concerns,* 25-26.
[95] Porter, *Compendium of Methodism,* 149.
[96] Jarrell, *Methodism on the March,* 169.
[97] On the front page of the first issue of the *Christian Advocate* was a two column article entitled, "Finley, the Methodist Missionary, and the Converted Indian Chiefs."
[98] "The Christian Advocate, 1826-1926," *Christian Advocate,* CI (1926), 1094. The centennial number of the *Advocate* issued September 9, 1926, contains a mine of material devoted to a hundred years of Methodism.

CHAPTER VI

MISSIONARY EFFORTS AMONG THE INDIANS

Little is recorded of the work of early ministers among the savages of the frontier; yet, the scanty accounts of their endeavors show that they possessed courage and vision. The urgent need and immense field for missionary work among the Indians had been recognized for many years by the Methodist Episcopal Church, but preachers were too scarce and church coffers too poor to permit any early redivision of the program of evangelization.

The organization of the Missionary Society of the Methodist Church in New York in 1819[1] induced the General Conference of 1820 to discuss the formation of auxiliaries to the parent society. The primary intention was "to assist the several Annual Conferences to extend their missionary labors throughout the United States and elsewhere."[2] This action gave the necessary impetus for the beginning of extensive labor in regions heretofore untouched. The Ohio Conference, however, had made considerable progress among the Indians before 1820. In 1815, while Marcus Lindsey was conducting a meeting in Marietta, Ohio, a dissipated Virginia mulatto, John Stewart, was going by and was attracted by the preacher's voice.[3] While standing in the door of the meetinghouse, Stewart fell under the power of the message and was converted. He now felt that duty called him to the Northwest to preach among the Indians. After working independently with several tribes during the years 1816 and 1817, he was admitted on trial by the Ohio Conference in 1817.[4] When the conference met in Cincinnati in 1819, it sent James Montgomery to Stewart's aid and placed this work, known as the Wyandot Mission, under the direction of James B. Finley. The mission flourished for a number of years and continued with

---

1 F. M. North, "The Foreign Missions of the Methodist Episcopal Church," *Christian Advocate,* CI (1926), 1147-1148.
2 "Extract from the Report of the Committee on Missions," *Meth. Mag.,* VII (1824), 279. For the manner in which Methodism has extended its missions see W. J. Sassnett, "The Relation of the Church to Missions," *Meth. Rev.* (Nashville, 1852), VI, 259.
3 Some writers said that Stewart was on the way to the river to drown himself when he heard Lindsey's voice. See McTyeire, *History of Methodism,* 577; Finley, *Sketches,* 388.
4 *Minutes,* I, 302; *Journals of the Ohio Conference,* 152.

varying degrees of success until the Wyandots sold their lands in Ohio and moved to the present Wyandot County, Kansas.[5]

Following closely on the heels of the formation of the Wyandot Mission, the Tennessee Conference also received the missionary urge. The *Journal* recorded the missionary work in the following manner:

> Thomas L. Douglass informed the Conference that $27.00 had been placed in his hands by Brother Cunnyngham for missionary purposes, and moved that said money be equally divided between the preachers who may be appointed to the mission in Jackson's Purchase.[6] Seconded, voted and carried.[7]

A committee was appointed to consider the subject of missions, and to report its recommendation. The report, which was adopted, directed the president of the conference to send missionaries to Jackson's Purchase, recommended the organization of the proposed Missionary Society Auxiliary, and made it obligatory upon the presiding elders and preachers in charge to gather funds for the support of the missionaries appointed by the conference.[8] Two missionaries were appointed to that part of Jackson's Purchase[9] which was contained in the states of Kentucky and Tennessee. Hezekiah Holland was sent from the Kentucky Conference[10] to serve in the northern portion of the

---

5 For this first Methodist Indian Mission see four books of J. B. Finley, *History of the Wyandot Mission at Upper Sandusky, Ohio, under the Direction of the Methodist Episcopal Church* (Cincinnati, 1840); *Life Among the Indians* (Cincinnati, n. d.); *Autobiography; Sketches.* Also, see "The Wyandot Mission," ch. iv, Sweet, *Circuit Rider Days Along the Ohio;* Emil Schulp, "The Wyandot Mission," Ohio Arch. and Hist. Soc. *Publications,* XV (1906), 163-181.

6 Opened by the Treaty of Jackson's Purchase ratified January 9, 1819, between the United States and the Indian chiefs. On October 19, 1818, the United States purchased from the Chickasaws the title to all lands north of the southern boundary of the state of Tennessee, west of the Tennessee River, south of the Ohio, and east of the Mississippi for $300,000, payable in fifteen annual installments. Treaty found in *Treaties between the United States of America and the Several Indian Tribes from 1778-1837* (Washington, 1837), 261-264. This cession embraced some seven milion acres, an area that exceeds that of eight states, and a dozen in population. Smith, *History of Kentucky,* 507-508. Neither Schouler nor McMaster mention the Purchase.

7 *Journal of the Tennessee Conference,* quoted by McFerrin, *Methodism in Tennessee,* III, 182

8 *Ibid.,* III, 183-184. See letter from Enoch George to editors of the *Methodist Magazine,* V (1822), 476.

9 See the "Chickasaw Treaty of 1818," ch. xi, Williams, *Beginnings of West Tennessee.*

10 At the General Conference of 1820 the Tennessee Conference was divided into the Kentucky and Tennessee conferences. At the annual conference above mentioned the actual division had not been made and hence the appointment of a missionary from the Kentucky Conference.

AMONG THE INDIANS

Purchase and Lewis Garrett from the Tennessee Conference to the lower portion.[11]

Garrett began his work on November 10, 1820, and continued alone until October, 1821, when Andrew J. Crawford was sent to his assistance. The division of the Purchase into only two missions indicates the extent of the field of labor for these pioneers of the Gospel. The North Mission included all the land lying north of the south fork of the Obion River. It extended as far south as the sectional line running east and west near Dougherty's land office, and lying partly in Tennessee and partly in Kentucky, it reached east and west from the Tennessee to the Mississippi River. The South Mission lay south of the sectional line mentioned above and extended to the southern boundary of Tennessee, and from the Tennessee River to the Mississippi, including the waters of the Forked Deer, Hatchie, and Beech rivers, and the headwaters of the Obion and Sandy. In spite of the extent of territory to be covered, the work progressed rapidly.[12] Thomas L. Douglass[13] and John McGee were present at the second quarterly meeting held in the South Mission on June 9-10, 1821. Six hundred attended on Sunday, June 10, to witness probably the first sacrament administered in West Tennessee.[14]

The South Mission was in time formed into two circuits; one designated as Forked Deer, and the other as Beech. The two contained thirty-three preaching places and 155 members. Preachers stationed on the Dover Circuit in Kentucky took care of the North Mission with its 131 members.[15] For the year 1820-1821 Garrett received ninety-two dollars and Crawford, forty-six. At the conference of 1821, a new district was created; Garrett was appointed to superintend both missions. Andrew J. Crawford was assigned to the Forked Deer Circuit; Jacob Hearn, to the Broad River; and Abraham Overall, to the

---

11 *Minutes,* I, 368; Redford, *Western Cavaliers,* 36-37.
12 "An Account of the Mission in Jackson's Purchase, under the Direction of the Tennessee Conference, in a Letter to Bishop McKendree," *Meth. Mag.,* VI (1823), 234. This letter from Lewis Garrett is one of the very few records of this missionary endeavor.
13 At that time presiding elder of the Nashville District.
14 "An Account of the Mission in Jackson's Purchase," *Meth. Mag.,* VI (1823), 234.
15 *Idem; Minutes,* I, 382. The Dover Circuit of 1820 is called the Tennessee in 1821. *Minutes,* I, 364, 382.

Big Hatchie. To the North Mission was sent Benjamin Q. Crouch and Lewis Parker.[16] The following amounts were received by Garrett and his South Mission itinerants for the year 1822:

	From Contributions	From Deficiency Fund
Garrett	$100.29½	$70.50
Crawford	27.00	3.00
Hearn	18.87½	11.12½
Overall	16.00	14.00
	$162.17	$98.62½[17]

From this work came the pathetic but uncomplaining words of Lewis Garrett, "Under these circumstances we have the opportunity of administering to our necessities, as long as our private funds will enable us to do so; then we must desist; but our reward is with our Master."[18] It is not surprising that President William Henry Harrison, who knew the West as few men ever did, remarked that the Methodist preachers in the early days were forced to live as though they had taken the vows of poverty.[19] In spite of hardships, sufferings, and scanty pay, the work continued. Every year brought additional converts; missionary zeal flourished; new districts were formed; preachers were added—all that makes a successful missionary endeavor was made manifest here.[20]

The *Minutes* for 1822 are the last that show a missionary to Jackson's Purchase. That year found in the four circuits of the North and South missions a total of 576 white members and sixty-six colored.[21] There is no report as to how many of the 576 were Indians as the *Minutes* list the Indians as white. The mission was absorbed into the newly formed Duck River District. In 1824 the Kentucky Conference formed the Tennessee Mission (in the Kentucky portion of Jackson's Purchase) and sent to it the aged Benjamin Ogden.[22] Within the two full years of the

---
16 *Ibid.*, I, 387.
17 "An Account of the Mission in Jackson's Purchase," *Meth. Mag.*, VI (1823), 236.
18 *Idem.*
19 Finley, *Sketches*, 143.
20 See "Fourth Anniversary of the Missionary Society of the Methodist Episcopal Church," *Meth. Mag.*, VI (1823), 277.
21 *Minutes*, I, 387, 406.
22 Redford, *Western Cavaliers*, 38; *Minutes*, I, 452.

mission's existence it grew from a one-man circuit to four circuits, with nearly six hundred members. These congregations were cared for by five preachers,[23] who met every requirement laid down by Douglass. In writing to the editors of the *Methodist Magazine* before the mission was organized, Douglass said that men were needed "who, renouncing ease and worldly prospects, devoted to God, and His Church, and qualified for the divine work in which they were engaged, will spread the word of life; and by uniting precept with example, they will plant the standard of Immanuel, and diffuse light to thousands in regions where darkness now reigns."[24]

On January 11, 1821, Bishop McKendree appointed William Capers as "missionary in South Carolina Conference, and to the Indians."[25] This appointment marked the definite launching of a great missionary campaign on the part of the whole church. Few men have been better equipped for the work to which they were assigned than was Capers. Born near Charleston, in 1790, of a respectable South Carolina family; a graduate of the State College; thirty-two years of age at the time of his appointment,[26] he measured up to every desired characteristic for the inauguration of a new undertaking. Capers secured sites for two missions in the Creek Nation. The plan was to organize two schools, the principal one to be called Asbury and located one mile west of the Chattahoochee River, near the present Fort Mitchell; the second, to be called McKendree Mission, was also to be in Alabama near the town of Tuckabatchee on the Tallapoosa River.[27] The latter appeared in the *Minutes* only once;[28] but the Asbury Manual Labor School was established, and, under very trying circumstances, it lasted until 1830.[29]

In the spring of 1822 Richard Riley, a prominent half-breed of the Cherokee Nation, living twelve miles south of Fort Deposit, Alabama, requested Rev. Richard Neeley, assistant on

---

23 *Ibid.*, I, 368, 386, 406.
24 *Meth. Mag.*, III (1820), 316.
25 West, *Methodism in Alabama*, 367-369; *Minutes*, I, 353, 369.
26 Paine, *William McKendree*, 375-381; O. P. Fitzgerald, *Centenary Cameos* (Nashville, 1885), 205-210.
27 West, *Methodism in Alabama*, 367-370.
28 *Minutes*, I, 388.
29 West, *Methodism in Alabama*, 370-383.

the Paint Rock Circuit (Huntsville District) to preach at his (Riley's) house. To this request Neeley gave a ready consent. With the aid of Rev. Robert Boyd who also traveled in that circuit, Neeley formed a society of thirty-three members, of which Riley was recognized and accepted as the leader. The society continued with such enthusiasm that William McMahon, presiding elder, thought it wise to hold a quarterly meeting at Paint Rock. The success of this work was reported to the conference which met in Greene County, Tennessee, in October, 1822. The report recommended that a mission should be established in the Cherokee Nation, that a missionary should be appointed to reside in the neighborhood of Riley in order to preach to the Indians and instruct the children, that a committee should be appointed to receive subscriptions and solicit donations for the support of the mission.[30] For a committee to arrange the mission, the conference chose William McMahon, Thomas Stringfield, and Andrew J. Crawford. The last was appointed missionary, his services in West Tennessee having furnished him with the necessary training and experience.[31] Crawford arrived at Riley's in December and made known his mission. Riley approved Crawford's plans for the establishment of a school for the Indian children. The school commenced on December 30 with twelve children, and the enrollment soon increased to twenty-five. Gratifying results came quickly; in a short time the children learned to spell words of three and four syllables. Both preaching and teaching met some opposition from the Indians, but this hostile feeling soon passed away.[32]

On July 31, 1823, a two-day camp meeting was begun. The natives had provided comfortable accommodations and an abundance of food for the preachers and all others present. Some of the Indians had traveled a distance of sixty miles to observe and participate in the white man's religious festival. These Indians

---

[30] "Report of the Tennessee Conference Missionary Society," *Meth. Mag.,* VII (1824), 192. This report was made by T. L. Douglass who was chairman of the missionary committee. Also, see West, *Methodism in Alabama,* 384-386.

[31] McFerrin, *Methodism in Tennessee,* III, 206, 208; *Minutes,* I, 411, 428; "History of Methodist Missions," *Meth. Mag.,* XIV (1832), 252; West, *Methodism in Alabama,* 385.

[32] "Report of the Tennessee Conference Missionary Society," *Meth. Mag.,* VII (1824), 192; West, *Methodism in Alabama,* 386.

were imbued with a co-operative spirit, for it is recorded that although few of them could speak or understand the English language, twenty-five adults and twenty children were baptized and received into the church.[33] After the preachers had declared the meeting at an end, twenty or thirty Indians came into the altar[34] and requested the preachers to instruct them how "to get favor with the Great Spirit." In his enthusiasm one of the wealthiest of the Indians proposed that all should pool their provisions and continue at the camp ground as long as the food lasted.[35]

Other work was also conducted among the Cherokees. About one hundred miles from the mission at Riley's, a Mr. Coody lived near Ross' post office on the main road from Nashville to Georgia. In 1822 he invited two Methodist ministers to preach at his house. A society was soon afterwards formed, which by 1824 had eighty members. Coody requested a missionary for that section of the Cherokee Mission and offered to give one hundred dollars a year toward supporting him.[36] At the Tennessee Annual Conference of 1823, this Indian mission was divided into the Upper and Lower Cherokee. Nicholas D. Scales was sent to the northern section, lying wholly within the limits of Tennessee. Since it had been requested that Richard Neeley be returned to his old work, he was again placed in charge of the southern section. Scales and Neeley each taught a school of fifteen or twenty pupils, who made progress in acquiring knowledge of the English language and skill in its use, grammar, reading, and writing. Besides their teaching duties, the missionaries preached every Sunday and from two to five times in the week.[37]

---

33 Contrast this statement, the source of which is Douglass' report, *Meth. Mag.*, VII (1824), 193, with a letter from Enoch George. *Ibid.*, V (1822), 476. West, *Methodism in Alabama*, 387, says: "One of the preachers, through an interpreter, pointed out to them Jesus."
34 The altar, twenty to thirty feet square, was inclosed with rails, with a door at each corner. The ground was covered with straw on which to kneel. Only mourners and personal workers were admitted into the altar. The men were allotted one side and the women the other. See *Meth. Mag.*, IV (1821), 192; McFerrin, *Methodism in Tennessee*, I, 337.
35 "Report of the Tennessee Conference Missionary Society," *Meth. Mag.*, VII (1824), 193. In 1825 the United Foreign Missionary Society received from the Cherokees $9.95 for mission work among the Osages with the statement that "the Bible tells us to do good to our enemies and I believe that the Osages are the greatest enemies the Cherokees have." *Christian Instructor*, I (1824), 127.
36 "Report of the Tennessee Conference Missionary Society," *Meth. Mag.*, VII (1824), 194-195; West, *Methodism in Alabama*, 388.
37 "Cherokee Mission," *Meth. Mag.*, IX (1826), 36; West, *Methodism in Alabama*, 388.

At the General Conference of 1824 the Committee on Missions reported that striking success had attended their exertions for the past four years. Requests for workers were so numerous that the conference scarcely knew where to place the few available men to the best advantage. The committee felt that "Missions among the Indians ought to be prosecuted with increased vigor.... While Zion is lengthening her cords and enlarging her borders, she ought also to strengthen her stakes; otherwise her entanglements will be her weakness." The Quadrennial Report of the Missionary Society influenced the adoption of a very important resolution:

> That Annual Conferences, where a missionary is employed, shall determine that amount necessary for the support of the mission. The president of the conference shall have authority to draw upon the treasury for that amount. The Bishops shall have the right to draw on the Society for only sums at disposal of the Society.[38]

When the Tennessee Conference met in the autumn of 1824, Thomas L. Douglass made a report on the work. A committee was appointed to estimate the amount necessary to support a missionary for the year. The report said: "The expenses necessary for a married man and his family, $350; and for each single man, $150. Contingent expense, $100."[39] Just how much money the Tennessee Conference advanced for the upkeep of the Indian mission is not known. The new regulation, however, provided substantial aid, and "The Quadrennial Report of the Managers of the Missionary Society of the Methodist Episcopal Church" shows that from May 21, 1823, to April 23, 1824, the Tennessee Conference was paid five hundred dollars for the support of missions.[40]

In 1827, five years after its inception, the Cherokee Mission numbered 675 converts with seven stations and as many preachers,[41] among whom were John B. McFerrin[42] and Turtle Fields,

---
38 "Extract from the Report of the Committee on Missions," *Meth. Mag.*, VII (1824), 277-278.
39 In McFerrin, *Methodism in Tennessee*, III, 270.
40 Reprinted in *Meth. Mag.*, VII (1824), 279-280.
41 *Minutes*, I, 553.
42 A report from the *New York Observer* on the missions among the Cherokees is quoted in Wardle, *Sunday School Movement*, 58; and in "Methodist Missions

a native Cherokee.⁴³ After 1830 the membership steadily decreased chiefly because of a reduced field for labor caused by Indian migrations, inroads of white people, and the presence of other denominations. Four years later the mission was discontinued. By a treaty made December 29, 1835, to which an additional article was added by a treaty, March, 1836, the Cherokees ceded to the United States all the lands which they owned or claimed east of the Mississippi.⁴⁴ Work among the Cherokees continued in the Holston region until 1838 when the last preacher to the Indians was transferred to Arkansas.⁴⁵

Another important missionary endeavor among the Indians was that of Alexander Talley who was commissioned in 1827 to preach among the Choctaws of northern Mississippi.⁴⁶ To the Mississippi Annual Conference which met in Tuscaloosa, Alabama, on Christmas Day, 1828, Talley took a delegation of Choctaw converts, one of whom made a report of the work which had been done among them.⁴⁷

In view of the successes recounted, and the even greater ones that followed these early efforts,⁴⁸ it seems that William H. Milburn under-estimated, or perhaps misstated, the actual existing conditions when he wrote:

> The Indian must perish. We cannot absorb him, cannot render him an integral part of our own society. We drive him further Westward, fight him, murder him with whiskey. Our missionaries labor amongst his deceiving bands with praiseworthy perseverance, but with an utter hopeless prospect. God's law is against him. He cannot enter into our laborious civilization, he cannot live amongst it; and he must needs disappear.⁴⁹

Among the Cherokees," *Meth. Mag.* (London), 1827, p. 338. McFerrin was assigned a circuit four hundred miles in circumference, which he covered once a month. Joseph Blackbird, a full-blood Indian, was McFerrin's interpreter. Fitzgerald, *John B. McFerrin*, 69.
43 For a sketch of Turtle Fields, first Cherokee employed as a Methodist itinerant, see West, *Methodism in Alabama*, 399.
44 William MacDonald, *Jacksonian Democracy* (New York, 1906), 179-181.
45 West, *Methodism in Alabama*, 398.
46 *Minutes*, I, 555.
47 McTyeire, *History of Methodism*, 580-581.
48 For a study of the Cherokee missions, chiefly after 1828, see G. F. Mellen, "Early Methodists and the Cherokees," *Meth. Rev.* (Nashville, 1917), LXVI, 476-487.
49 W. H. Milburn, *The Pioneers, Preachers, and People of the Mississippi Valley* (New York, 1860), 457-458. See Theophilus Armenius, "A Descriptive View of the Western Country," *Meth. Mag.*, III (1820), 387, for changes wrought among native inhabitants.

Joshua Soule, who was much more intimately acquainted with the Indian situation and condition than was Milburn, gave a different estimate of the work accomplished among the Indians.

> We have a thousand living monuments before us, in proof that the gospel of Jesus Christ is suited to every condition of the human race; that whether man may be savage or civilized it is the gospel of his salvation.[50]

---

[50] "Extract of a Letter from the Rev. Bishop Soule," *Meth. Mag.*, XI (1828), 79.

CHAPTER VII

THE NEGRO AND THE METHODIST CHURCH

While missionaries of the church were engaged in carrying its benefits to the Indians they also found it necessary to face the question of religious welfare of the negro whose relationship to the white man was different from that of the Indian.

"The legislation of the Methodist Church, on slavery, has been distinguished from the beginning by suspension, repeal, change or modification, and exemption of the members in a number of the states from the operation of her laws." These words were written in 1850 by Bishop Joshua Soule of the Methodist Episcopal Church, South.[1] In spite of this thoroughly truthful statement the Methodists "have always, and justly, considered their Church as a pioneer anti-slavery institution."[2]

Before John Wesley sailed for America his attention was called to slavery by a letter from Dr. John Burton of Oxford, who, on September 28, 1735, wrote to him: "One end for which we were associated was the conversion of negro slaves. As yet, nothing has been attempted in this way; but a door is opened . . . the harvest truly is great."[3] Wesley's early fight against slavery took concrete form when he wrote into the General Rules of 1743 for the organization of the English societies the rule which forbade "The buying or selling the bodies and souls of men, women, or children, with an intention to enslave them."[4] In his *Journal* of February 12, 1772, Wesley recorded:

> I read a very different book published by an honest Quaker, on that execrable sum of all villanies, commonly called the Slave-trade. I read of nothing like it in the heathen world, whether ancient or modern. And it infinitely exceeds, in every

---

1 Joshua Soule, "The Methodist Church and Slavery," *Meth. Rev.* (Nashville, 1908), LVII, 638. Reprinted from the *Texas Wesleyan Banner*, October 12, 1850. Although a New Englander, Bishop Soule followed the southern wing of the Methodist Church.
2 J. H. Norwood, *The Schism in the Methodist Church*, 1844: *A Study of Slavery and Ecclesiastical Politics* (New York, 1923), 9. See, also, L. C. Matlack, "Our Past and Present Relations to Slavery," *Meth. Rev.* (New York, 1868), L, 252-263.
3 Quoted by Luke Tyerman, *Life and Times of the Rev. John Wesley* (3 vols., New York, 1872), I, 109-110.
4 L. C. Matlack, *The Antislavery Struggle and Triumph in the Methodist Episcopal Church* (New York, 1881), 58.

instance of barbarity, whatever Christian slaves suffer in Mahometan countries.[5]

On February 26, 1791, only four days before his death, he wrote to William Wilberforce, who had just offered in the British parliament a resolution for the abolition of slavery in the West Indies: "Go on in the name of God, and in the power of his might, till even American slavery (the vilest that ever saw the sun) shall vanish away before it."[6]

A series of excerpts from the *Journal* of Francis Asbury, the real founder of American Methodism, reveals his opposition to slavery and reflects the change that the Bishop saw manifesting itself in the congregations: 1776, "After preaching . . . I met the class, and then met the black people, some of whose unhappy masters forbid their coming for religious instruction. How will the sons of oppression answer for their conduct, when the great Proprietor of all shall call them to account!" 1780, "O Lord, banish the infernal spirit of slavery from thy dear Zion." 1784, "I pity the poor slaves. O that God would look down in mercy, and take their cause in hand!" 1794, "O, when will liberty be extended to the sable sons of Africa?" 1796, "My spirit was grieved at the conduct of some Methodists, that hire out slaves at public places to the highest bidder, to cut, skin, and starve them." 1798, "O! to be dependent on slaveholders is in part to be a slave, and I was free-born. I am brought to conclude that slavery will exist in Virginia perhaps for ages; there is not a sufficient sense of religion nor of liberty to destroy it." 1801, "What absurdities will not men defend! If the Gospel will tolerate slavery, what will it not authorize?"[7]

Freeborn Garrettson, one of the very ablest native-born preachers and a mighty force in the early period, turned from a slaveholder to an antislavery advocate. He was sent to North Carolina in 1777, and there, after reviewing conditions, he wrote in his *Journal*: "Many times did my heart ache on account of the slaves in this part of the country, and many tears did I shed both

---

5 John Wesley, *The Journal* (4 vols., New York, 1907), III, 461.
6 John Emory (ed.), *The Works of the Reverend John Wesley* (7 vols., New York, 1835), VII, 237.
7 Asbury, *Journal*, I, 187, 374, 482; II, 246, 326, 367; III, 10.

in Virginia and Carolina, while exhibiting a crucified Jesus to their view."[8]

Of all the early important ministers of the church in America George Whitefield was the only one who was not wholeheartedly in opposition to slavery. He went so far as to approve the action by which Georgia was changed from a free to a slave colony. Slaves were purchased for the plantation connected with Whitefield's orphanage, Bethesda, near Savannah,[9] in a desire "to make their lives more comfortable, and lay a foundation for breeding up their posterity in the nurture and admonition of the Lord."[10] John Wesley's opinion that American slavery was "the vilest that ever saw the sun" and Francis Asbury's prayer that "the infernal spirit of slavery" would be banished from "dear Zion" are truly indicative of the attitude of primitive Methodism toward enslavement of the negro.

Antislavery workers appeared in East Tennessee with the first settlers. A letter signed by Thomas Embree was addressed to the people of Tennessee and published in the *Knoxville Gazette,* January 23, 1797. His purpose was to call a meeting of citizens of Washington and Greene counties in order to form abolition societies in that section of the state and to labor for the

> relief of such persons as are illegally held in bondage; to effect their relief by legal means alone, without any intention to injure the rights of individuals . . . not to take negroes from their legal masters and set them free, as some have vainly imagined; but by lawful means to vindicate the course of such of the human race as are lawfully entitled to freedom, either by mixed blood or any other cause.

Since no further information has been found the society was probably never formed. In 1814, however, an organized antislavery effort was begun in Tennessee by the formation of a society in Jefferson County. A year later, on the twenty-first

---

8 Quoted from the *Journal of Freeborn Garrettson* by Grissom, *Methodism in North Carolina,* 227. See, also, McTyeire, *History of Methodism,* 310.
9 E. E. Hoss, "Elihu Embree, Abolitionist," *American Historical Magazine* (Nashville, 1897), II, 113. See, also, *The Works of the Reverend George Whitefield* (2 vols., London, 1771-1772), II, 404-405; John Gillies, *Memoirs of Rev. George Whitefield* (Middletown, Connecticut, 1829), 45-48; G. G. Smith, *History of Methodism in Georgia and Florida from 1785-1865* (Macon, Georgia, 1881), 22.
10 *The Works of the Reverend George Whitefield,* II, 405. Letter dated March 22, 1751.

of November, delegates from different societies met in a state convention at the Lick Creek Meeting House of Friends in Greene County and formed a permanent organization under the name of the "Manumission Society of Tennessee." The outstanding leader here was the Quaker minister, Charles Osborn, who also aided in the formation of many branch societies. The Rev. John Rankin of the Presbyterian Church assisted. A considerable number of Methodists and Baptists were identified with the different societies and materially aided in the work. During the first three decades of the nineteenth century the membership of antislavery societies in the slave states usually exceeded that of the free states. As late as 1827, East Tennessee alone contained nearly one-fifth of all antislavery societies in the United States and nearly one-sixth of the total membership.[11]

Slavery had found its way into American Methodism during the Revolution when the administration of the church was in the hands of young and inexperienced members, themselves born and reared in the midst of slavery. All the annual conferences from 1776 to 1787 were held in slave states, and no appointments of ministers were made north of New Jersey between 1777 and 1783.[12]

In the Methodist annual conferences of 1780 action was taken disapproving slavery.[13] At the time (1784) of the organization of the church in America laws were enacted regulating slavery. The minutes giving these regulations were as follows:

> Question 12. What shall we do with our friends that will buy and sell slaves?
> If they buy with no design than to hold them as slaves, and have been previously warned, they shall be expelled; and permitted to sell on no consideration.
> Question 13. What shall we do with our local preachers who will not emancipate in the states where the laws admit it?

---

11 For discussion of this subject see A. E. Martin, "The Anti-Slavery Societies in Tennessee," *Tenn. Hist. Mag.*, I (1915), 261-281. According to Theodore Roosevelt (*Winning of the West*, VI, 9-12) the early settlers in Tennessee actually abhorred slavery.

12 W. W. Sweet, *The Methodist Episcopal Church and the Civil War* (Cincinnati, 1912), 16; Matlack, *Antislavery Struggle and Triumph*, 54-55; Norwood, *The Schism in the Methodist Church*, 14.

13 *Minutes*, I, 12.

Try those in Virginia another year and suspend the preachers in Maryland, Delaware, Pennsylvania, and New Jersey.[14]

This legislation against slavery was the high-water mark reached in early Methodist opposition. "In the judgment of the Conference there was something peculiar to those exempted states, either in their laws, their usages, or their geographical position, which so far remedies the moral evils of slavery as to render it innocent and consequently no bar to communion in the Church of God."[15] There appears little doubt that due to the views and force of Asbury, Coke,[16] and Wesley, the rigid legislation of 1784 was thrust upon an unwilling conference and was possibly received by a generally hostile membership. The mark was set too high; the legislation was too drastic. In not more than six months, it was found necessary "to suspend the execution of the minute[s] on slavery till the deliberation of a future conference . . . ."[17] To this suspension, however, was added an inconspicuous footnote which stated, "We do hold in the deepest abhorrence the practice of slavery; and shall not cease to seek its destruction by all wise and prudent means."[18]

In 1796 another stand was taken, which, although not as strong as the one of 1784, readily demonstrated that the desire for emancipation was still existent among the more powerful members of the clergy.[19] In that year to the General Rule on slavery was appended a prohibition against "buying and selling the souls and bodies of men."[20] In the General Conference of 1800[21] a measure was passed requiring the annual conferences to present to the legislatures of the slaveholding states addresses urging the enactment of laws for the emancipation of slaves. In 1804 slaveholding under certain conditions was granted to church members, and the states of North Carolina, South Carolina, and Georgia were exempted from the rules. Four years

---

14 *Ibid.*, I, 20.
15 Soule, "The Methodist Church and Slavery," *Meth. Rev.* (Nashville, 1908), LVII, 638.
16 For Coke's opposition to slavery see Drew, *Life of Thomas Coke*, 180-183.
17 *Minutes*, I, 24. See Matlack, *Antislavery Struggle and Triumph*, 254.
18 *Minutes*, I, 24.
19 See the question and answer regarding slavery. *Ibid.*, I, 28.
20 *Discipline* for 1796, quoted in Sweet, *Methodist Church and Civil War*, 17.
21 A Methodist general conference meets every four years.

later the General Conference was in a compromising mood, for all that related to slaveholding among members was forever removed. The authority to govern members who engaged in slave-trade was given to each annual conference, and, furthermore, an expurgated edition of the *Discipline* was prepared for the South Carolina Conference in which the rule on slavery was omitted.[22] Contemporary with this conference the Western Annual Conference took occasion to pass a law concerning slavery.[23] Asbury recorded the action: "We made a regulation respecting slavery; it was, that no member of society, or preacher, should sell or buy a slave unjustly, inhumanly, or covetously.... Where the guilt was proved the offender to be expelled."[24]

The minutes of the first session of the Tennessee Conference, meeting in 1812, contain the following action—typical of the treatment of the slave question: "Leven Edney, recommended from Nashville Circuit; his character examined and approved, Learner Blackman being security that he'll set his slave free, when practicable."[25] Many promised and gave "security" but never found it "practicable" to liberate their slaves. A stringent manumission act had been passed in Tennessee in 1801 permitting the owner to free his slave only on presentation of a petition which showed reasons acceptable to two-thirds of the court.[26] By 1816 sentiment had changed to such an extent that the Tennessee Conference went on record as believing that slavery was a moral evil, "But as the laws of our country do not admit of emancipation without a special act of the Legislature ... we cannot adopt any rule by which we can compel our members to liberate their slaves."[27] In other regions,[28] also, the church, finding its former restrictions becoming incompatible with state legislation, was forced to substitute expediency for a moral question. In 1817 the old question was once again before the law—

---

22 *Journals of the General Conference,* I, 41, 63, 93.
23 *Journal of the Western Conference,* 148.
24 Asbury, *Journal,* III, 290.
25 Quoted in McFerrin, *Methodism in Tennessee,* II, 261; Price, *Holston Methodism,* II, 212-213.
26 Edward Scott, *Laws of the State of Tennessee, Including Those of North Carolina Now in Force in this State* (2 vols., Knoxville, 1821), I, 714-715.
27 Quoted by McFerrin, *Methodism in Tennessee,* II, 401; Price, *Holston Methodism,* II, 215.
28 Kentucky, for example. See Redford, *Methodism in Kentucky,* II, 502.

makers of the church in Tennessee. This time a report was adopted which repealed every law regarding slavery hitherto passed by the Tennessee Conference. Rules were enacted that would have placed stringent restrictions on the sale and purchase of slaves had not each regulation been flanked and supported by a provision that rendered it forceless.[29] A year later the church legislation removed the ban of slaveholding from all members except ministers or candidates for the ministry by the adoption of the resolution to "receive the printed rule on Slavery, in the form of Discipline, as full and sufficient on that subject."[30]

In 1820 the General Conference resumed control of slavery, and the right to regulate slave traffic was withdrawn forever from the annual conferences.[31] This transfer of legislation was largely the result of a movement instigated by a minority party in the Tennessee Conference of 1819 led by Henry Bascom, a confessed sympathizer with slavery,[32] who desired to remove the power of restricting slave traffic from the hands of the local conference, where the antislavery party at that time happened to occupy the "exact ground upon which the Northern abolition party in the Church" stood, to the authority of a larger and more removed judiciary.[33] The minority was determined not to find itself faced by rigid restrictions in slaveholding. In 1824— for the last time until 1860—the section on slavery was amended.[34]

The Methodist Church, however, did not relinquish its care for the negro's spiritual needs. These it fostered in a manner which was satisfying to both master and slave. The blacks and

---

[29] For reprint of 1817 slavery rules of Tennessee Conference see McFerrin, *Methodism in Tennessee*, II, 462-466; Price, *Holston Methodism*, II, 240-243. "When men or women determined to own slaves, it was easy to make it appear . . . according to the rules of justice or mercy . . . ." McFerrin, II, 467.
[30] *Ibid.*, III, 19-20. The General Conference of 1808 removed from the *Discipline* all regulations on slaveholding among private members. *Journals of the General Conference*, I, 93. See, also, L. C. Matlack, *The History of American Slavery and Methodism* (New York, 1849), 33.
[31] *Journals of the General Conference*, I, 205; Paine, *William McKendree*, 292.
[32] See the case of Dr. G. D. Taylor who was admitted (1819) as a traveling preacher oncondition that he would emancipate his slaves "when practicable." Henkle, *Life of Bascom*, 117-120; Redford, *Methodism in Kentucky*, II, 502-504.
[33] Henkle, *Life of Bascom*, 117-121.
[34] *Journals of the General Conference*, I, 294. "If the reader can discover any connection between the extirpation of slavery and these provisions, he is possessed of remarkable keenness of perception." Matlack, *American Slavery and Methodism*, 31. See, also, A. E. Martin, *The Anti-Slavery Movement in Kentucky Prior to 1850* (Louisville, 1918), 35.

whites met in the same building and heard the same sermon.[35] The mixed churches never troubled the slaveholder for the color line was political and social, but not religious.[36] Usually the back seats were set apart for the negro, or if it were a camp meeting he was placed behind the altar. Methodism had a peculiar attraction for the negro, because the emotional experience caught his fancy, and his soul responded to every song and shout.[37] The Baptist Church similarly attracted the negroes, whose imaginations were especially struck by the mode of baptism. To them immersion "is a palpable, overt act, that their imagination can take hold of."[38] The preacher particularly welcomed the negro to the camp meeting since he could be brought easily into a hypnotic condition, and from him the frenzy spread to the whites.[39]

The negro came so easily into the ranks of the church that no particular program of missionary work with his race was considered necessary before 1829. At this time, William Capers was sent to South Carolina to superintend two negro missions located on the Santee and the Ashley rivers.[40] There were 1,352 negro members in the Tennessee Conference in 1815, and this number had increased to 3,240 by 1820. The Mississippi Conference, formed in 1816, had almost three thousand negro members within nine years.[41]

Paradoxical as it may seem, in many northern cities the negro church-goers suffered unkind treatment at the hands of the whites who "even pulled them off their knees, while in the act of prayer and ordered them back to their seats."[42] As a result of such repeated actions, and after long deliberation, a

---

35 J. H. Caldwell, "The Relation of the Colored People to the Methodist Episcopal Church, South," *Meth. Rev.* (Nashville, 1866), XLVIII, 419-421. T. A. Kerley, "One Hundred Years of Missionary Operations in the Tennessee Conference," *Tenn. Conf. Jour.*, 1912, p. 159. For an interesting account of the relations between whites and blacks see R. Q. Mallard, *Plantation Life Before Emancipation* (Richmond, 1892).
36 J. C. Ballagh, *A History of Slavery in Virginia* (Baltimore, 1902), 114.
37 Grissom, *Methodism in North Carolina*, 284.
38 F. L. Olmsted (*A Journey in the Seaboard Slave States*, New York, 1856, p. 114) quoted a Virginia correspondent writing in the *New York Times* on the comparative strength and influence of the different denominations.
39 U. B. Phillips, *American Negro Slavery* (New York, 1918), 316-318.
40 W. M. Wightman, *Life of William Capers, D. D.* (Nashville, 1859), 291.
41 *Minutes*, I, 295, 366, 473.
42 Quoted by McTyeire, *History of Methodism*, 564, from the preface to the *Doctrines and Discipline of the African Methodist Episcopal Church*. This statement was signed by six negro bishops.

THE NEGRO AND THE CHURCH 99

large number of negro members seceded from a Philadelphia church and organized the African Methodist Episcopal Church in that city in the year 1816. Richard Allen, a self-liberated slave, was the first bishop of this new church.[43] This separate organization made no progress in the South until the Civil War severed the connection of the negro from the church of his master.

---

43 McTyeire, *History of Methodism*, 564-565; Porter, *Compendium of Methodism*, 163.

CHAPTER VIII

EFFORTS FOR A TEMPERATE SOCIAL ORDER

Methodism's early fight against liquor had much in common with its opposition to slavery. Both efforts opened with a flourish only to sag to the middle ground of compromise, and finally to be relinquished. The stand which the church took in opposition to drink was, however, remarkable in its boldness and aggressiveness when contrasted with the general and widespread use of distilled liquids.

Distilled liquors were used in excessive quantities by the early American.[1] His thirst was slaked by no ordinary draught. The eleven thousand dollar expenditure for wine and liquor made by Jefferson during his eight years as president was in keeping with the general indulgence in distilled spirits. In 1787 Andrew Ellicott, leaving on a four-month's surveying trip of the West, took for his party one hundred and seventy-six gallons of rum, sixty-four of whiskey, and sixteen of brandy. A general storekeeper in Georgia often sold as much as thirty pounds sterling worth of rum in a day. Frequently fifty men were drinking at the same time within a rod of his door[2]. Drunkenness was so prevalent in the Carolinas before 1800 that one of its historians called it an "endemic vice of Carolina."[3] Dr. Lyman Beecher declared that in 1812 the yearly consumption of distilled spirits was five gallons a person.[4] Five years later, newspapers in discussing the cost of intemperance set the mark at thirty-three million dollars.[5] Dr. Philip Lindsley, for twenty-six years presi-

---

1 McAfee, *Life and Times*, 233-234, 240-241; E. P. Fordham, *Personal Narrative of Travels in Virginia, Maryland, Pennsylvania, Ohio, Indiana, Kentucky; and of a Residence in the Illinois Territory*: 1817-1818 (ed. by F. A. Ogg, Cleveland, 1906), 180; Luccock, *The Story of Methodism*, 446; A. H. Noll, *History of the Church in the Diocese of Tennessee* (New York, 1900), 24; Asbury, "The Father of Prohibition," *American Mercury*, IX (1926), 345; Paxson, *The American Frontier*, 115; Bennett, "Pioneer Methodism in Virginia," *Meth. Rev.* (Nashville, 1888), V, 90; Hugh Williamson, *The History of North Carolina* (2 vols., Philadelphia, 1812), II, 204-205; McDonnold, *Cumberland Presbyterian Church*, 7; J. T. Christian, *A History of the Baptists in Louisiana* (Shreveport, 1923), 15, 121.
2 Channing, *History of the United States*, IV, 16-17.
3 David Ramsay, *The History of South Carolina from its First Settlement in 1670 to the Year* 1809 (2 vols., Charleston, 1809), II, 391. Ramsay felt that the "number of strictly temperate people is far short of what is generally supposed." *Ibid.*, II, 394.
4 Channing, *History of the United States*, V, 175, n. 2.
5 McMaster, *History of the United States*, IV, 53.

dent of the University of Nashville,[6] stated in a baccalaureate address delivered on October 3, 1827,[7] that nine-tenths of the criminals had been made by intemperance; sixty thousand of our citizens were each year destroyed directly by liquor or by diseases resulting from its use; and that Tennessee's expenditure for distilled spirits amounted to $1,250,000 annually.[8] Such enormous consumption undoubtedly had a large share in earning for Kentuckians the common description of "half horse, half alligator, tipped with snapping turtle."[9] Shortly before his death Asbury recorded in his *Journal*: "At Boling's we were greatly annoyed by a brigade of Kentuckians; can fiends be more wicked? The drunkards kept the house in an uproar."[10]

The important economic reason for the wholesale distilling of whiskey in the West was the common deficiency of all frontiers—the lack of means of transportation. People were unable to pay taxes from the sale of grain which would not bear portage. Almost by necessity they were driven to convert their farm products into a portable product by means of distillation.[11] A horse could carry barely four bushels of corn in the form of grain, but in the form of a distilled liquor the equivalent of twenty-four bushels might be transported to the Eastern markets. Jacob Young has told the story of a Methodist brother who sold some flour to several persons and took notes at the rate of twenty-six bushels of rye for each barrel of flour to be paid in rye after harvesting. When the rye was received it was converted into whiskey, and each bushel produced three gallons. The whiskey was sold to soldiers at three dollars a gallon. By these trans-

---

6 See Halsey, *Works of Philip Lindsley*, I, 11-62; III, 9-78, for a biographical sketch of this pioneer Western educator.

7 Before the student body of the University of Nashville.

8 Halsey, *Works of Philip Lindsley*, I, 181-182. For additional instances of Lindsley's fight against liquor see *ibid.*, I, 183-186, 293; III, 491, 506-508, 518-525.

9 McMaster, *History of the United States*, II, 578. From Natchez, Mississippi, John A. Quitman, later governor of the state, wrote his father a letter in 1822 which gives a typical description of drinking in river towns on the frontier. See J. F. H. Claiborne, *Life and Correspondence of John A. Quitman* (2 vols., New York, 1860), I, 71-72.

10 Asbury, *Journal*, III, 469.

11 Channing, *History of the United States*, IV, 138-139. The lack of transportation facilities and the open resistance to taxes provided the background and cause of the Whiskey Insurrectoin in Pennsylvania in 1794. H. M. Brackenridge, *History of the Western Insurrection in Western Pennsylvania* (Pittsburg, 1859) was written from the standpoint of one of the participants.

actions approximately two hundred dollars was cleared from each barrel of flour.[12]

In addition to the economic causes there were other reasons for the prevalence of huge quantities of liquor on the frontier.[13] People used it freely on all occasions; whiskey was the material means of celebrating a birth, a marriage, or any other occasion of importance.[14] Asbury felt that the preachers refrained from accepting drams;[15] but not all of the preachers were total abstainers.[16] Cartwright recorded instances of personal contact with drunken Baptist,[17] Seceder, Presbyterian, and Methodist preachers.[18] Lyman Beecher in his *Autobiography* described an ordination in Connecticut during which the ministers drank so often that the sideboard "with the spillings of water, and sugar, and liquor, looked and smelled like the bar of a very active grogshop."[19] This taste for drink was also prevalent among church members on the frontier where Cartwright found it a task to secure a committee of non-dram drinkers to try a Methodist preacher who had been drunk on several occasions.[20] Asbury, when passing through the South in 1795, wrote in his *Journal*: "Sunday. Was an awful day—perhaps the most awful I shall ever spend in this place .... This country improves in cultivation, wickedness, and stills; a prophet of strong drink would be acceptable to many of these people .... "[21]

Ardent spirits were used as a preventive of diseases such as agues and fevers. Alcohol was regarded as a necessity for

---

12 Young, *Autobiography*, 310.
13 In 1810 there were twenty-eight distilleries in Indiana Territory manufacturing 39,350 gallons a year. See Sweet. *Rise of Methodism*, 64.
14 Joseph Smith, *Old Redstone; or Historical Sketches of Western Presbyterianism and its Early Ministers* (Philadelphia, 1854), 251-265; Finley, *Autobiography*, 248-251; Cartwright, *Autobiography*, 212; Sweet, *Rise of Methodism*, 64; McAfee, *Life and Times*, 244-245; Drake, *Pioneer Kentucky*, 58, 83.
15 Asbury, *Journal*, II, 261.
16 Henry Wheeler, "Relations of the Methodist Episcopal Church to the Cause of Temperance," *Meth. Rev.* (New York, 1876), LVIII, 630-631.
17 Cartwright, *Autobiography*, 30, 113, 137-138. After taking in one who claimed to be a Baptist preacher, Cartwright decided to charge him for the night's lodging since he thought "it a bad sign for a preacher to smell very strong of whiskey." *Ibid.*, 137-138. "I have often seen it [whiskey] carried and used at large baptizings, when the ordinance was administered by immersion." *Ibid.*, 212.
18 *Ibid.*, 60, 85-86, 184-185, 214. Two of the Methodist preachers to whom Cartwright referred were delegates to the General Conference. When Bishop McKendree sent Cartwright on a private mission into the Red River Circuit in 1817, he dreaded the task for he knew that "there were about twenty talented local preachers" in that circuit who were participators in the evils of dram-drinking and extravagant dress. *Ibid.*, 182.
19 Quoted in Channing, *History of the United States*, V, 175.
20 Cartwright, *Autobiography*, 185.
21 Asbury, *Journal*, II, 261.

EFFORTS FOR TEMPERANCE

persons engaged in strenuous labor.[22] The making or drinking of whiskey was not considered disreputable. Camp meetings, preaching services, funerals, weddings, all were subject to the unexpected conduct of drinking men.[23] An idea of the tolerance adopted toward the use of liquor can be derived from the fact that the basements of the second and third Methodist churches in New York City were rented for the storage of ale and beer.[24] During the decade of 1820-1830, the *Christian Advocate* in quoting New York current prices included the quotation on brandy, whiskey, gin, and wine.[25]

The history of the temperance movement in Tennessee goes back to the beginning of the state. James Robertson, the "Father of Tennessee," declared "the conversion of grain into spirituous liquors is an unwarranted perversion, unservicable to white man and devilish for Indians"; and he expressed the hope that "there may never be any waste of grain by distillation, or waste of estates or ruin of soul by drinking liquor."[26] This statement from Robertson is not an attempt to convey the idea that temperance prevailed in Tennessee in those early days. The contrary must have been true since the opposition presupposes the existence of the evil.[27]

Wesley found drunkenness one of the most prevalent and outstanding evils of his day. The ravages of liquor excited him to action against its very existence. The bans on this subject have revealed many changes as follows:

> 1743. Wesley's original rule. Drunkenness, buying or selling spirituous liquors, or drinking them, unless in case of

---

22 S. W. Williams, *Pictures of Early Methodism in Ohio* (Cincinnati, 1909), 26. Thomas' *Almanac* for 1806 states that "the rum drunk by three hands in the haying season would purchase three calves or pay the taxes of a small farmer." See Channing, *History of the United States*, IV, 17, n. 2. See Drake, *Pioneer Kentucky*, 56, for drinking at corn huskings.
23 Finley, *Autobiography*, 252, 350; Cartwright, *Autobiography*, 270-271; Brunson, *Western Pioneer*, I, 250-253, 283-285; II, 30.
24 Luccock, *The Story of Methodism*, 466; Deets Pickett, "The Methodists and the Drink Traffic," *Christian Advocate*, CI (1926), 1223.
25 *Ibid.*, CI (1926), 1221-1223, 1226, 1230.
26 Quoted in Taylor, *Historic Sullivan*, 196. Alexander Hamilton in his report on the "Public Credit" in 1790 stated that consumption of ardent spirit "is carried to an extreme which is truly to be regretted, as well in regard to the health and morals, as to the economy of the community." Quoted in Channing, *History of the United States*, V, 175, n. 1.
27 See the *Christian Instructor*, I (1825), 91-92, for "A Bill of Mortality" alleging that of the twenty-nine people who died in Knoxville, Tennessee, in 1824, ten died from intemperance.

extreme necessity.

    1789. Drunkenness, buying or selling spirituous liquors, or drinking them.

    1790. Drunkenness, or drinking spirituous liquors, unless in cases of necessity.[28]

In 1780 the Baltimore Conference went on record in the following manner:

> Question 23: Do we disapprove of the practice of distilling grain into liquor? Shall we disown our friends who will not renounce the practice?
> Answer: Yes.[29]

Three years later even higher ground was taken when the following was added to the *Minutes*:

> Question 11: Should our friends be permitted to make spirituous liquors, sell or drink them in drams?
> Answer: By no means. We think it wrong in its nature and consequences; and desire all our preachers to teach the people by precept and example to put away this evil.[30]

By 1796 the custom of retailing spirituous liquors had become so offensive as to require a special law by the General Conference meeting in that year. A new section was added to the *Discipline* which set forth in no uncertain terms that

> If any member of our Societies retail or give spirituous liquors, and anything disorderly be transacted under his roof on this account, the preacher who has the oversight of the circuit shall proceed against him, as in the case of other immoralities, and the person accused shall be cleared, censured, suspended, or excluded according to his conduct, as on other charges of immorality.[31]

In the General Conference of 1812 James Axley from Tennessee offered the motion that no stationed or local preacher should retail spirituous or malt liquors without forfeiting his ministerial character. This included fermented liquors in the

---

28 Quoted in Wheeler, "Relations of the Methodist Episcopal Church to the Cause of Temperance," *Meth. Rev.* (New York, 1876), LVIII, 629.
29 *Minutes*, I, 12.
30 *Ibid.*, I, 18.
31 Quoted in Wheeler, "Relations of the Methodist Episcopal Church to the Cause of Temperance," *Meth. Rev.* (New York, 1876), LVIII, 632.

same class with distilled spirits. After several attempts to carry the motion it was vigorously voted down. It is significant that this aggressive measure was sponsored by a son of the frontier, the chief characteristic of which is generally thought to be revealed in the inclusive phrase, moral laxity. Yet James Axley and his frontier churchmen were much in advance of the mind of the General Conference. Four years later Axley presented the same resolution which he had introduced in 1812, with the elimination of the reference to malt liquors, and to the regulation in this form there was little opposition. This law is a sad comment on the state of the times. By 1820 the per capita production of distilled spirits in the country was over seven gallons. At the Baltimore Conference of that year a resolution was offered that no member of the church should distill ardent spirits without forfeiting his standing. The motion was indefinitely postponed.[32]

In spite of the failure of the resolution of 1820, Methodism had taken a bold stand against an evil that pervaded all classes of society.[33] Some writers claim that "the Methodist Church was the first Christian Church since the apostles which forbade the use of spirituous liquors as a beverage and their sale for such purpose."[34] If the frontier did consume more liquor than the older settled regions, in the same proportion it provided a formulative environment which produced reformers such as Finley, Young,[35] Cartwright, and Axley. The names of Axley and Cartwright were intimately woven into the very woof and warp of the church in Tennessee and Kentucky. An extract from Finley is illustrative of the work accomplished in the West by Methodist preachers as social reformers:

> Frequently I would pledge whole congregations, standing upon their feet, to the temperance cause; and during my rounds I am certain the better portion of the entire community became the friends and advocates of temperance, and on this circuit alone, at least one thousand had solemnly taken the pledge of

---
[32] *Journals of the General Conference*, I, 106, 107, 168, 239.
[33] Eddy, "Influence of Methodism upon the Civilization and Education of the West," *Meth. Rev.* (New York, 1857), XXXIX, 287-288.
[34] Wheeler, "Relations of the Methodist Episcopal Church to the Cause of Temperance," *Meth. Rev.* (New York, 1876), LVIII, 630. See Bacon, *History of American Christianity*, 206.
[35] For Young's fight against whiskey see his *Autobiography*, 274-276, 310.

total abstinence. This was before temperance societies were heard of in this country.³⁶

Among these advocates of temperance were many whose names were not so familiar, but whose obscurity did not lessen their enthusiasm. One of these was James O'Cull, "a perfect son of thunder," who, while preaching one day on drunkards and whiskey and whiskey-makers, said, "I would to God all the stills in the world were in one, and that was in the belly of hell."³⁷ Archibald McElroy was also a great champion of the cause, and on one occasion in 1811 was asked to preach in the Court House of St. Clairsville, Ohio. Before he entered the building he had seen several drunken men lying about the town; he also had seen some hogs running loose in the streets contrary to the laws of the city. This he felt was a splendid opportunity to preach against drunkenness. He advised the people to preserve order and to obey the laws against loose hogs, "for," said he, "many of your citizens are in the habit of getting drunk, and lying in the streets and alleys, and are in danger of being eaten up by the hogs."³⁸

Peter Cartwright was an inveterate enemy of whiskey, and his encounters with it in camp meetings were numerous. On one occasion he found a keg of whiskey hidden in the bushes. He brought it into the camp and placed it under a guard. When rumors came to him that the rowdies were planning to stone him during the night in order to recapture their keg, he beat them at their game by lying awake, and at the first noise pelting rocks so furiously into the group that they ran away.³⁹

James Axley, tall, raw-boned, and awkward, probably deserves the honor of being the most famous preacher-opponent of liquor who lived on the frontier.⁴⁰ For many years he lived in East Tennessee, which, at that time, was regarded as a profitable locality for producing peach brandy, and for the free dispensation of it.⁴¹ Axley's famous temperance sermon in that section

---
36 Finley, *Autobiography*, 251.
37 Brooks, *Life and Times*, 120.
38 Young, *Autobiography*, 275-276.
39 Cartwright, *Autobiography*, 270-271.
40 Finley, *Autobiography*, 241.
41 Finley, *Sketches*, 238-240.

is illustrative of the work of the leaders against the curse, and is typical of the sermons that were so popular.

TEXT: 'Alexander the coppersmith did me much evil: the Lord reward him according to his works,' 2 Timothy, iv, 14.

Paul was a traveling preacher, and a bishop, I presume, or a presiding elder at least; for he traveled extensively, and had much to do not only in regulating the societies, but also in sending the preachers here, there, and yonder. He was zealous, laborious, would not build on another man's foundation, but formed new circuits, where Christ was not named, 'so that from Jerusalem, and round about unto Illyricum, he had fully preached the Gospel of Christ.' One new place that he visited was very wicked—Sabbath-breaking, dancing, drinking, quarreling, fighting, swearing, etc., abounded; but the word of the Lord took effect; there was a powerful stir among the people, and many precious souls were converted. Among the subjects of that work there was a certain noted character, Alexander by name, and a still-maker by trade; also, one Hymeneus, who was his partner in the business. Paul formed a new society, and appointed brother Alexander as class-leader. There was a great change in the place, the people left off their drinking, swearing, fighting, horse-racing, dancing, and all their wicked practices. The stills were worked up into bells and stew-kettles, and thus applied to useful purposes. The settlement was orderly, the meetings were prosperous, and things went well among them for some time. But one year they had a pleasant spring; there was no late frost, and the peach crop hit exactly. I do suppose, my brethren, that such a crop of peaches was never known before. The old folks ate all they could eat, the children ate all they could eat, the pigs ate all they could eat, and the sisters preserved all they could preserve, and still the limbs of the trees were bending and breaking. One Sunday, when the brethren met for worship, they gathered round outside of the meeting-house, and got to talking about their worldly business—as you know people sometimes do, and it is a mighty bad practice—and one said to another, 'Brother, how is the peach crop with you this year?' 'O,' said he, 'you never saw the like; they are rotting on the ground under the trees; I don't know what to do with them.' 'How would it do,' said one, 'to still them? The peaches will go to waste, but the brandy will keep; and it is very good in certain cases, if not used to excess.' 'I should like to know,' said a cute brother, 'how you could make brandy without stills?' 'That's nothing,' replied one, 'for our class-leader—brother Alexander—is as good a still-maker as need be, and brother Hymeneus is another, and, rather than see the fruit wasted, no doubt they would make a few.' The next thing heard on the subject was a hammering in the class-leader's shop; and soon the stills in every brother's orchard were smoking, and the liquid poison streaming. When one called on another the bottle was brought out, with the remark, 'I want you to taste my new brandy; I think it is pretty good.' The guest, after tasting once, was urged to repeat, when, smacking his lips, he would reply, 'Well, it's tolerable; but I wish you would come over and taste mine; I think mine is a little better.' So they tasted and tasted till many of them got about half-drunk, and I don't know but three-quarters. Then the very devil was raised among them; the society was all in an uproar, and Paul was sent for to come and settle the difficulty. At first it was difficult to find sober, disinterested ones enough to try the guilty; but finally he got his committee formed; and the first one he brought to account was Alexander, who pleaded not guilty. He declared that he had not tasted, bought, sold, or distilled a drop of brandy. 'But,' said Paul, 'you made the stills, otherwise there could have been no liquor, no one could have been intoxicated.' So they expelled him first, then Hymeneus next, and went on for compliment, till the society was relieved of all still-makers, distillers, dram-sellers, and dram-drinkers, and peace was once more restored. Paul says, 'Holding faith and a good conscience; which some having put away, concerning faith have made shipwreck; of whom is Hymeneus and Alexander; whom I have delivered unto Satan, that they may learn not to blaspheme.'[42]

The early Western itinerants were not alone in their fight for temperance. From the church organs such as the *Christian Instructor* came ringing denunciations of the use of liquor, of which the following is a fair example:

> Among the various evils which stalk amid the haunts of men, there is one demon of destruction, whose march, sure as time, impetuous as the cataract, and merciless as the grave, desolates the fairest valley of the universe, and lays prostrate the noblest structure of creation. At his approach, the towering wing of genius is paralyzed, the torch of reason becomes extinct, the fire of ambition expires, the smile of philanthropy

---

[42] This sermon may be found in Finley, *Sketches,* 238-240.

EFFORTS FOR TEMPERANCE 109

is lost in the cloud of conscious degradation, the rose of health is blanched, the lustre of the eye is dimmed, and the flowers of domestic love, hope and joy are withered forever. His name is Intemperance.[43]

Asbury found it necessary to expel many of the preachers who failed to refrain from the use of whiskey.[44] Many suppositions may be drawn from the highly interesting fact that ten of the twenty-one preachers expelled from 1817 to 1825 were from the Tennessee, Ohio, Missouri, Mississippi, and Kentucky conferences.[45]

There was also a negligible fight against the use of snuff and tobacco in this early period. The organizations within the church, such as the bands and class meetings, were supposed to include the most circumspect—abstainers from snuff taking and dram drinking—both evils, however, had crept in.[46] Even the Presbyterian "blue stockings" were not safe from the expectoration of tobacco juice according to one of Philip Lindsley's anecdotes. He related in 1831 to a Tennessee audience how

> The other day at church, a well-dressed young fellow, while standing up on prayer time and leaning over into my pew, so wantonly besprinkled every part of my premises with his tobacco distillations, as fairly to put all devotion out of countenance, and made me wish for the Amen, as impatiently as ever did hungry urchin during his puritan papa's long grace over a Thanksgiving Day's dinner.[47]

Against the use of tobacco James Axley stood out again as the leading preacher-reformer of his period in the entire West. He once delivered a sermon on tobacco much to the discomfort of Judge Hugh Lawson White[48] who was sitting near the front with an uncommonly large quid in his mouth. According to White's account of his embarrassment,

> Axley's singular manner and train of remark strongly arrested my attention. While he was stirring to the right and

---
43 From "A Fragment," *Christian Instructor*, I (1825), 156-157.
44 Asbury, "The Father of Prohibition," *American Mercury*, IX (1926), 345.
45 Examine *Minutes*, I, 287-470.
46 See Wheeler, "Relations of the Methodist Episcopal Church to the Cause of Temperance," *Meth. Rev.* (New York, 1876), LVIII, 631.
47 Halsey, *Works of Philip Lindsley*, III, 623-624.
48 Later United States Senator from Tennessee.

left, hitting those things that he was not going to talk about, my curiosity was busy to find out what he could be aiming at. I was chewing and spitting my large quid with uncommon rapidity, and looking up at the preacher to catch every word and every gesture—when at last he pounced upon the tobacco, behold, there I had a great puddle of tobacco spit! I quietly slipped the quid out of my mouth, and dashed it as far as I could under the seats, resolved never to be found chewing tobacco in the Methodist Church.[49]

Axley also had a sermon that he preached occasionally called "Sermon on Abomination," in which he included masonry, slavery, whiskey, tobacco, and fashions. Once in the course of this sermon he turned to tobacco, and, since smoking was done chiefly by the women, he recited for them a poem which he had written.

> Tobacco is an Indian weed,
> And from the devil did proceed;
> It spoils a woman, burns her clothes,
> And makes a chimney of her nose.

An old woman was so incensed by his reproach that she left the assembly, and as she passed from the room, turned around and said, "I wish to God I had my pipe, I would smoke this minute for spite."[50]

In the midst of a class meeting Axley once inquired of a pious German as to the condition of his tobacco crop. Upon receiving the answer "Very well," Axley teasingly said, "You are the meanest people in this neighborhood I ever saw. It's all tobacco, tobacco, and you do not raise corn enough to feed my horse when I come round." Whereupon the German retorted, "Brudder Axley, if you vill not deach your horse to eat derbacker, dat is not our vault. Deach him dis, and den ve give him blenty." "Never!" said the indignant Axley. "If Bob was to chew tobacco, I would never speak to him again."[51]

Many preachers, as well as members were constant users of the weed. One Indiana circuit rider is said to have spat twice a minute throughout the course of his sermon so that "the pulpit

---

[49] Quoted in Finley, *Sketches*, 245. Also, see Redford, *Methodism in Kentucky*, II, 439-442.
[50] *Ibid.*, II, 421-423.
[51] *Ibid.*, II, 424-425.

was as filthy as a stable" at the close of his address.⁵² During his entire life, Bishop McKendree maintained an opposition to the "needless self-indulgence" in the use of tobacco. On September 30, 1790, he wrote in his diary:

> Rode to Brother Andrew's, and met a few people. The Christians were not engaged, and the sinners looked impudently wicked. I strove to be faithful, and was plain in class-meeting. Some seemed a little moved, but so soon as meeting was over and they were out of class, one had a pipe, another was after a chew of tobacco, and the women with their snuff boxes, until my soul was grieved.⁵³

With the passing of years the steady fight that these early Western reformers made against intemperance achieved noteworthy success. Alfred Brunson declared that at a camp meeting in Ohio a man remarked that so many had turned Methodist that the price of whiskey had fallen from fifty cents to twenty-five cents a gallon.⁵⁴ Beyond question the Methodist itinerant was instrumental in reducing the per capita consumption of liquors fifty per cent between the years 1810 and 1840.⁵⁵ The bettered conditions on that ever changing frontier attest the value of Methodism's heroic war against "the two great potentates of this Western World—whiskey [and] brandy" which Asbury once feared would be "the ruin of all that is excellent in morals and government."⁵⁶

---

52 Wright, *Hawkers and Walkers*, 150.
53 Quoted in Paine, *William McKendree*, 104. For a sermon preached by a Virginia Methodist preacher against tobacco see Edwards, *Life of Childs*, 83.
54 Channing, *History of the United States*, V, 175, n. 2. For the attitude of Methodists toward temperance in a slightly later period see Sweet, *Circuit Rider Days in Indiana*, 69, 147; Redford, *Western Cavaliers*, 83-85.
55 Brunson, *Western Pioneer*, I, 188.
56 Asbury, *Journal*, II, 481. See, also, *ibid.*, III, 391; Henry Wheeler, *Methodism and the Temperance Reform* (New York, 1882), 63; Bangs, *History of the Methodist Church*, II, 352.

CHAPTER IX

THE ORGANIC STRUCTURE OF THE CHURCH

American Methodism inherited from John Wesley a well developed form of church government. The structural organization of the church, however, grew in complexity with its missionary, educational, and reformatory endeavors. Indeed there was something peculiar in the organization of a church which was adaptable to the various localities, adjustable to different situations, and flexible to individual needs. The secret of its success lay not in the members, but in the mechanical organization which gave motivation to its activities.

Autocracy and democracy were strangely blended in the polity and doctrine of the early organization of Methodism. The structure of the church was autocratic, and hence, was "conspicuously out of accord with the democratic stirring of the times."[1] This characteristic was inherited largely from the church father John Wesley, who, as a thorough-going autocrat, refused to countenance any interference with the plans which he had made or might make. His course was so despotic that more than half of the seven hundred preachers whom he received into the Methodist ministry left it early in life. In expelling one Alexander McNabb, the Methodist preacher at Bath in 1780, Wesley wrote, "Whoever, therefore, violates these conditions, particularly that of being directed by me in the work, does *ipso facto* disjoin himself from me . . . . So long as any preacher joins with me, he is to be directed by me in his work."[2]

The entire history of the origin of the Methodist Episcopal Church in America and its subsequent growth is a peculiar fluctuating contest between the oligarchic and democratic forces which strove for control. These two characteristics first met in serious encounter in 1784, at which time the Methodist societies in America separated themselves from the domination of John

---

[1] Mode, *Frontier Spirit*, 123. For Methodism in the period of the Revolutionary War see *ibid.*, 383; Grissom, *Methodism in North Carolina*, ch. iv; Bacon, *History of American Christianity*, 202; Duvall, *The Methodist Church and Education*, 14-15; Van Tyne, "Influence of the Clergy and of Religious and Sectarian Forces on the American Revolution," *Amer. Hist. Rev.*, XIX (1913-1914), 44-64.

[2] Quoted in Luccock, *The Story of Methodism*, 196-197.

THE CHURCH STRUCTURE 113

Wesley. The conference at Baltimore in that year began the actual organization of the church government.

This conference of 1784[3] was in one respect the first general conference, since all the annual conferences were supposed to be represented there; however, no provision was made for a future session until 1792. During this interim, the conferences were meeting annually[4] in small units. General church measures were submitted by the superintendents to one annual conference after another. A majority of all was necessary for the validity of any measure.[5] In an effort to improve this highly unsatisfactory mode of legislative procedure, Bishop Asbury devised the council plan,[6] "a retrograde movement . . . toward centralization of power,"[7] by which a small group of presiding elders would actually run the church.[8] Once again democracy in religion had suffered a serious infringement upon its rights. Wesley's dominance had passed only to be supplanted by that of Asbury. Coke's absence from the sessions of the Council both in 1789 and in 1790 gave Asbury an absolute veto on all proposed church legislation,[9] since the presiding elders were the appointees of the bishops and were removable at their pleasure. According to Lee the proceedings of the council "gave such dissatisfaction to our connection in general, and to some of the traveling preachers in particular, that they were forced to abandon the plan."[10]

The General Conference, containing preachers representing all of the circuits, assembled in Baltimore on November 1, 1792. One day was devoted to consideration of the rules of the house, and on the second day, James O'Kelly, a presiding elder of the Southern District of Virginia, brought forward an amendment proposing that

---

3 Until 1784 Wesley was the only recognized authority in the Methodist societies. Kerley, *Conference Rights*, 99. See Tipple, *Francis Asbury*, ch. v, for a splendid discussion of the Christmas Conference.
4 Three in 1786 and 1787, six in 1788, eleven in 1789, fourteen in 1790, thirteen in 1791, and seventeen in 1792. *Minutes*, I, 24, 26, 29, 32, 35, 39, 43. The *Minutes* can only be depended upon for those conferences appointed and not those held.
5 Stevens, *History of Methodism*, 195.
6 See Lee, *Methodists in the United States*, 149-155; Tigert, *Constitutional History of Methodism*, ch. xiv; McTyeire, *History of Methodism*, 402-403.
7 Kerley, *Conference Rights*, 105.
8 Luccock, *The Story of Methodism*, 247.
9 Tigert, *Constitutional History of Methodism*, 244.
10 See Lee, *Methodists in the United States*, 150-159.

After the bishop appoints the preachers at Conference to their several circuits, if anyone think himself injured by the appointment, he shall have liberty to appeal to the Conference and state his objections; and if the Conference approve his objections, the bishop shall appoint him to another circuit.[11]

The proceedings of this conference were never printed in separate minutes but were included in the next edition of the *Discipline*.[12] The motion, intended as a blow to the administration of Asbury, was lost by a large majority, and immediately O'Kelly announced that his connection with the conference was thereby terminated. O'Kelly carried with him some followers, among whom was William McKendree, who with the others "obtained liberty to return home without giving notice as to their ulterior purposes." To McKendree, O'Kelly unfolded his plan of "a republican, no slavery, glorious Church! Bishop Asbury was a pope; the General Conference was a revolutionizing body; the Bishop and his creatures were working the ruin of the Church to gratify their pride and ambition!"[13]

At this Baltimore conference it was decided that hereafter the conferences were to meet quadrennially and that in 1796 all traveling preachers who were itinerants of two years length were eligible for membership in it.[14] In 1808 the delegated general conference was provided for—the membership of which was composed of one member for every five members of each annual conference. These representatives should have traveled at least four years from the time they were received on trial.[15] The first delegated general conference met in New York City on May 1, 1812, and adjourned twenty-one days later. This began an unbroken line of four year conferences to which delegates were elected by a fixed ratio and to which body even bishops were accountable.[16]

At first the traveling preachers met in what were known as district, later to be called annual, conferences.[17] In 1785, when

---
11 *Ibid.*, 178.
12 Tigert, *Constitutional History of Methodism*, 257.
13 Paine, *William McKendree*, 123.
14 Tigert, *Constitutional History of Methodism*, 163.
15 *Journals of the General Conference*, I, 95.
16 Milburn, *Ten Years of Preacher Life*, 69.
17 For origin and development of the annual conference begun by Wesley in 1784 see McTyeire, *History of Methodism*, 211; Luccock, *The Story of Methodism*, 102-103.

three annual conferences were held, the caption of the minutes was changed from *Minutes of Some Conversations between the Preachers in Connection with the Rev. Mr. John Wesley* to that of *Minutes Taken at the Several Annual Conferences of the Methodist Episcopal Church*. A typical procedure of the annual conferences was conducted in the form of questions, as follows:

Questions:
1. Who are admitted on trial?
2. Who remain on trial?
3. Who are admitted into full connection?
4. Who are the deacons?
5. Who have been elected and ordained elders this year?
6. Who are the superintendents and bishops?
7. Who have located this year?
8. Who are the supernumerary preachers?
9. Who are the superannuated and wornout preachers?
10. Who have been expelled from the connection this year?
11. Who have withdrawn from the connection this year?
12. Were all the preachers' characters examined before the Conferences?
13. Who have died this year?
14. What numbers are in Society?
15. Where are the preachers stationed this year?
16. When and where shall our next Conference be held?[18]

At the close of each conference the presiding bishop would read out the list of appointments which changed the location of the major portion of the preachers. Frequently appointments were made from prejudice and favor; many of the clergy would be sent to circuits to which they were ill-suited, and of which they had no knowledge. At a conference held at Hopkinsville, Kentucky, no bishop was present, and the president *pro tem* was one of the leaders of the antislavery party with whom Henry Bascom was not at all a favorite. Whether this circumstance had any influence in the making of appointments or not, great astonishment was expressed when the president read, "Madison Circuit, Henry B. Bascom." It seemed very singular that a man widely known as a great pulpit orator should be sent to the most

---
18 *Minutes*, I, 5, 21, 152-164.

remote and inaccessible section in the whole conference;[19] it was perhaps more singular that a man who had already spent seven years in the itineracy should be continued in that position. But appointments were not always made to everybody's satisfaction nor was the conduct of the appointees always decorous. At the Tennessee Conference of 1821, two preachers were publicly reprimanded for having swapped circuits with the giving and taking of "boot" in the trade.[20]

The quarterly conference which had jurisdiction over the circuit was composed of the traveling and local preachers, exhorters, leaders, and stewards. For the church members this was the great festival in which Methodist social ties were strengthened and extended. The exercises continuing from Saturday morning through Sunday were largely spiritual. During these days there were almost incessant sermons, prayer meetings, sacraments, or love feasts. Where there were no church buildings the quarterly meetings, or two-day meetings, were held at a private home. Usually a double log cabin was chosen, the men occupying one side and the women the other. The programs varied according to the occasion, but the general plan was materially the same. The presiding elder opened the exercises with a sermon followed by an afternoon meeting of the conference officers. In the evening a sermon was followed by an exhortation. The first cock's crow was the signal for arising; breakfast was finished before eight, for at that time the Sunday services were inaugurated by a love feast to which only members of the church were admitted. After an appropriate hymn and a prayer, the leader explained briefly the nature of the feast and gave whatever advice he thought necessary. Some one would then strike the chord or note of an old familiar song, in which the whole gathering joined. Following this song, there would be testimonials interspersed with songs and shouts.[21] At eleven o'clock the ordinance of baptism preceded the sermon, and the communion of the Lord's Supper concluded the noon meeting. So lengthy was the day's program that

---

19 Henkle, *Life of Bascom*, 126-127. For treatment of Burke, Brunson, and Bascom see Sweet, *Circuit Rider Days Along the Ohio*, 54.
20 McFerrin, *Methodism in Tennessee*, III, 198-199; Price, *Holston Methodism*, II, 286.
21 Sullins, *Recollections*, 65-66; Porter, *Compendium of Methodism*, 468-469; John Tevis to Editors, *Meth. Mag.*, VI (1823), 351.

one writer has stated that on several occasions it was five o'clock before they tasted the second meal of the day. In the evening the last sermon was delivered, and when the call was made for converts, it was not uncommon for hundreds to come into the altar. Day-break on Monday usually found the people on their way home.[22]

The class meetings were organized for the purpose of indicating the spiritual temperature and for ascertaining the religious character of the church members.[23] As a local organization it was designed especially as a supplement to the itinerant system which made little provision for pastoral work.[24] The object of the societies was to provide for a smaller working unit, for the privilege of close communion, and for the expression of personal testimonials and experiences. It was the original plan for the membership to be limited to twelve, but this soon was discarded because of the lack of efficient leaders. The position of class leader has been termed "the nursery of the preachers,"[25] for here the duties of leader prepare the laymen for transference to the ministry. The leader first attempted to visit each member every week, but this proved impossible.[26] It was then decided to hold weekly meetings at a designated place, and only on the absentees did the leader then call.[27] A strict attendance was required, and at the meetings each member was checked on the roll book as "A", "P", or "D"—absent, present, or distant.[28]

---

[22] I have followed rather closely the quarterly meeting plan given by Milburn, *Ten Years of Preacher Life*, 54-56. For a highly interesting account of a meeting of a later period see J. V. Watson, *Tales and Takings, Sketches and Incidents* (New York, 1856), 363-373; Williams, *Early Methodism in Ohio*, 54-57.

[23] John Miley, *Class Meetings* (Cincinnati, 1859), 55, 166-168, 170; W. M. Punshon, *Sermons* (New York, 1860), 21-42; Cartwright, *Autobiography*, 519; Finley, *Autobiography*, 179, 194.

[24] Sassnett, "Theory of Methodist Class Meetings," *Meth. Rev.* (Nashville, 1851), V, 275-276; M. M. Henkle, *Primary Platforms of Methodism or Exposition of the General Rules* (Louisville, 1851), 102-103; J. W. Alexander, "The Sunday School in its Relation to the Church," *Meth. Rev.* (Nashville, 1890), IX, 520-521.

[25] Henkle, *Primary Platforms*, 100; Bangs, *History of the Methodist Church*, I, 247; J. W. Boswell, *A Short History of Methodism* (Nashville, 1901), 525; Redford (*Methodism in Kentucky*, II, 232) said that Benjamin Durham who immigrated to the District of Kentucky in 1781 "bears the distinguished honor of having been the first class leader in the West." The laity in the church has had its heroes. See F. R. Hill, "Heroes among the Laity in the Early History of Tennessee Methodism," *Tenn. Conf. Jour.*, 1912, pp. 117-127.

[26] For duties of the class leader see "Class Meetings," *Meth. Rev.* (Nashville, 1849), III, 578-586. An interesting history of a class leader of Lambeth Chapel, London, England, is that by Edward Corderay, *Father Reeves, The Model Class Leader* (Nashville, 1854). Also, see *A Memoir of Mr. William Carvossa, Sixty Years a Class Leader in the Wesleyan Methodist Connection* (Nashville, 1873).

[27] Miley, *Class Meetings*, 51, 201; Porter, *Compendium of Methodism*, 48.

[28] Sullins, *Recollections*, 67.

The requirements of membership were rigorous. Although the English custom of issuing admittance tickets to those whose spiritual status made them eligible for the close and inner communion of the classes was little used in America, the requirements were no less strict in the young country.[29]

The rules which governed membership forbade indulgences and excesses of any kind—particularly swearing, fighting, drinking, unbecoming conversation, and ornamental dress. Pride and the use of superfluous ornaments were grounds for excluding a woman from the societies. The rules said that none was to be admitted to the classes who "wear high heads, or enormous bonnets, ruffles, or rings."[30] Those who violated the rules were dropped as useless members[31] The membership was constituted as so many watchers over each other individually;[32] the demoralizing influences were thus warded off, and the necessary spiritual encouragement was provided.[33] So exacting were the class meetings that one member became so restless that he left the room by way of the chimney. Hatless, he jumped on the back of his horse and rode five miles without stopping. When he reached home, his wife inquired if the Indians were after him. His answer was "Worse than Indians."[34] In truth, the class furnished the militant spirit which looked after the welfare of the church during the time that elapsed from one visit of the traveling preacher to another.[35]

Yet the class meeting did not adequately provide for the intimate, personal communion which some desired. Consequently, three or four of the most religious men or women met together for a free and candid expression of their temptations, faults, and spiritual joys. Thus was the inner circle or band organized;

---

29 Porter, *Compendium of Methodism*, 49.
30 Quoted by Gewehr, "Factors in the Expansion of Methodism," *Journal of Religion*, VIII (1928), 109.
31 Miley, *Class Meetings*, 73; Cartwright, *Autobiography*, 188-189, relates an interesting occurrence in which a woman was ejected from a class meeting by force. He once ordered a young man's hair to be cut when he appeared at a camp meeting with his hair roached back in the "newest Nashville fashion." *Ibid.*, 141-142.
32 Sassnett, "Theory of Methodist Class Meetings," *Meth. Rev.* (Nashville, 1851), V, 277.
33 "Class Meetings," *Holston Messenger*, III (1828), 81-82.
34 Carr, *Early Times*, 128-129.
35 Porter, *Compendium of Methodism*, 50. For additional information see O. P. Fitzgerald, *The Class Meeting* (Nashville, 1898); McTyeire, *History of Methodism*, 201-203.

the sexes were separated, with the married or single men, and the married or single women together in a group.[36] As the years passed, the class meetings, love feasts, and bands lost their place in the church,[37] and as early as 1828 the *Holston Messenger* contained an article deploring the situation.[38]

The guidance and control of the various organizations of the church was placed in the hands of certain specified officers. Question 26 of the *Discipline* of 1784 asked, "What is the affair of a superintendent?" (this office was termed bishop after 1788),[39] and the answer was given:

> To ordain superintendents, elders, and deacons; to preside as a moderator in our Conferences; to fix the appointments of the preachers for the several circuits; and in the intervals of the Conference, to change, receive or suspend preachers, as necessity may require; and to receive appeals from preachers and people, and decide them.[40]

The first person to bear the official title of presiding elder was William McKendree in the appointments of 1797. By 1786 the elders, appointees of the bishops, had been given as their duties the administering of the sacrament and other rites and also of exercising within their own districts, during the absence of the bishops, the powers that were vested in their superiors.[41] On several occasions the general conference was thrown into a semi-panic over the matter of depriving the bishops of the right to appoint the presiding elders. The last notable contest occurred at the General Conference of 1820. Scarcely had the conference opened before the presiding elder question, a left-over from the previous conference, came up for discussion. The resolution was to have the elders elected by the conference instead of being chosen by the bishops. McKendree was absent from one business

---

36 J. M. Buckley, *A History of Methodists in the United States* (New York, 1896), 85; Sullins, *Recollections*, 65-66. For origin of love feast see McTyeire, *History of Methodism*, 200-210.
37 "Old Methodism," *Meth. Mag.*, XIX (1837), 212-229; Sassnett, "Theory of Methodist Class Meetings," *Meth. Rev.* (Nashville, 1851), V, 279-284. For a defense of class meetings see Emory, *Life of John Emory*, 207-211.
38 "Class Meetings," *Holston Messenger*, III (1828), 81-82.
39 *Minutes*, I, 29.
40 Quoted by Tigert, *Constitutional History of Methodism*, 207. See Bangs, *History of the Methodist Church*, II, 330-347, for duties of presiding elders. Also, see Paine, *William McKendree*, 339-345.
41 Tigert, *Constitutional History of Methodism*, 209, 213-216.

session because of illness, and at that time the question was put to a vote and was passed. The following morning Bishop McKendree returned to learn with chagrin of the business accomplished. In an hour's speech he attempted to show that this resolution was a strict violation of the constitution of the church. When a new vote was taken, the rule was suspended for a period of four years, and thus a sham compromise was effected.[42] The compromise of 1820 only postponed the inevitable break which came in 1830 in the organization of the Methodist Protestant Church.[43]

McKendree, now in the role of a despot, was championing all the virtures of the bishopric autocracy from which he had revolted and fled with O'Kelly in 1792. A radical spirit was permeating the church. Young preachers and the laity felt themselves capable of handling situations within their districts without the advice of a bishop.[44] When Asbury died, his dominating will being gone, a democratic people were rebelling against the dictates of a strong central head in church government.

The three orders in the ministry of the Methodist Episcopal Church were bishops, elders, and deacons. The bishops were elected by the general conference and held office for life. The local church, through the quarterly conference, was the only door of entrance into the ministry. Should this body grant admission, the candidate must serve an apprenticeship as a junior preacher, called a deacon, who worked under the direction of the senior preacher on the circuit. If he were placed in full charge of the circuit or society, he would be under the care of the presiding elder and would be endowed with all rights and privileges of the ministry except the administration of the Lord's Supper, in which he could assist the elder. At the close of the probationary period, ordinarily two years, the deacon was eligible, upon examination by the annual conference and through ordination by bishops and

---

42 Henkle, *Primary Platforms*, ch. xi; Young, *Autobiography*, 360-362; Cartwright, *Autobiography*, 196; *Journals of the General Conference*, I, 236; McTyeire, *History of Methodism*, 570-574; Price, *Holston Methodism*, II, 269-270.

43 In spite of this the presiding elders have continued to be the appointees of the bishops.

44 Jewell, *Methodism in Arkansas*, 375; L. E. Davis, "The Methodist Protestant Church," *Christian Advocate*, CI (1926), 1135-1136; E. M. North, "A Study of the Divisions of American Methodism," *Christian Advocate*, CI (1926), 1132-1133.

elders, to become a traveling elder possessed of all the powers of the ministry and charged with a lengthy list of duties.[45]

Besides these grades of the ministry there were others into whose care the work of each local society or church was given.[46] Each society had its trustees holding the property, and stewards in charge of the raising and spending of the money. The licensed exhorter and local preacher were potent aids in all church development. Local preachers were recruited from those in secular vocations who felt themselves unable to enter the permanent ministry, or from itinerants broken in health or fortune. This arrangement gave the church much talent which under any other arrangement would have been lost. Marriages, funerals, and baptisms fell to the hands of these local preachers when the itinerants were absent. Scattered throughout every corner of the West, the local preachers were instrumental in establishing churches in regions yet unvisited by the regular ministry. In many cases these local preachers were induced to enter the ministry, and so the office served as a valuable recruiting agency.[47] The exhorter was licensed merely to urge and evangelize rather than actually to serve as a preacher. Frequently he was graduated to the office of a local preacher, and from there to the traveling ministry.

Mere conversion at a camp meeting or preaching service by no means meant membership in the church, for as lax as some of the ways of conversion may have been, admission to the church was strict. From the beginning Wesley had held that for those seeking admission there was only one required condition and that was "a desire to flee from the wrath to come, and to be saved from their sins." In order to obtain membership one had to undergo a period of trial and instruction which was first set at two months, and was extended in 1789 to six months. The passing of the minimum probation, however, did not always insure membership; the applicant might be continued on trial, and if

---

45 Cutshall, *Training of the Ministry*, 49-50; Stevens, *History of Methodism*, 197; Tigert, *Constitutional History of Methodism*, 209; Jewell, *Methodism in Arkansas*, 16-17.

46 Faulkner, *The Methodists*, 307; Luccock, *The Story of Methodism*, 370-372.

47 Wilson, "Local Preachers," *Meth. Rev.* (Nashville, 1882), IV, 705-712; Finley, *Sketches*, 53, 62; Young, *Autobiography*, 77.

his case proved hopeless he was discontinued.[48] In this program of admission, a student of frontier religion contended that "the Methodist Church maintained a more careful supervision of its members than any other denomination."[49]

One writer has described the Methodist doctrine as "simple, understandable, practicable, preachable, traditional, unrooted in metaphysics, and devoid of philosophical subtlety."[50] Such a description would have meant little to a frontiersman. The Methodist qualities that pleased him above all others were those of the freedom of the will, and the individual responsibility in salvation. Through "experience" and "conversion" the penitent soul was divinely released from sin and was changed from a state of anxiety to that of certitude. The facilities which Methodism provided for the reinstatement of backsliders from grace made it especially attractive to unsteady members and prospective converts. Added to these features was the fact that no stringent doctrinal requirements were exacted for admission.[51]

Methodism's intelligible doctrines appealed to the frontiersmen and thousands became converts. It was, however, the autocratically centralized government of the church that held these same converts fast, promised to them a reward hereafter, and made of them powerful agencies in furthering the work of the church.

---

48 Henkle, *Primary Platforms*, 31-38, 70-90; Josephus Anderson, "Probationary Church-Membership," *Meth. Rev.* (Nashville, 1858), XII, 535-543; D. C. Kelley, "Methodist Church Membership," *Meth. Rev.* (Nashville, 1884), VI, 45-49.
49 Cleveland, *The Great Revival*, 50.
50 Cutshall, *Training of the Ministry*, 16-17. For Methodism's practicality see Nogler, *The Church in History*, 191; W. P. Lovejoy, "The Influence of Methodism," *Meth. Rev.* (Nashville, 1902), LI, 371; Jane Mesick, *The English Traveller in America, 1785-1835* (New York, 1922), 362-363.
51 W. J. Conoly, "The Catholicity of Methodism," *Meth. Rev.* (Nashville, 1916), LXV, 716-728; Charles Adams, "Wesley, the Catholic," *Meth. Rev.* (New York, 1851), XXXIII, 177-198.

CHAPTER X

METHODISM REACHES MATURITY

From its initial appearance in the Old Southwest, Methodism had proved itself equal to the emergencies of a new land. This success may be attributed to the fact that the church accommodated itself to the rapidly increasing population[1] and the demands of the people.

At the General Conference held in Baltimore, May 1-24, 1816, the Tennessee Conference was divided and two new conferences, the Missouri and the Mississippi, were formed. Thus delimited the Tennessee Conference now included the whole of Tennessee and about half of Kentucky. Upper Kentucky was a part of the Ohio Conference.[2] In the first year these two new divisions reported thirty circuits and 5,114 members—a partial indication of how much they had been needed. The proceedings of this Baltimore conference included several important issues which indicated the manner in which the church was trying to meet the exigency of the times. Two new bishops, Enoch George and Robert Richford Roberts, were elected. A striking advance toward a better clergy was made when a ruling was passed which provided for a course of reading and study for all candidates for the ministry.[3] This rule was the first educational legislation of the church as a governing body.[4] A committee which had been selected to act on the slavery question reported that "the evil appears to be past remedy" and that "to bring about such a change in the civil code as would favor the cause of liberty is not in the power of the General Conference."[5]

In the fall of 1816, the newly formed Tennessee Conference met at Franklin, with Bishop McKendree as presiding officer and Thomas L. Douglass as secretary.[6] A membership of 19,401 was reported from the circuits; this was a decrease in membership of over three thousand from the previous year—a loss

---

1 Between the years of 1810 and 1820 Tennessee advanced in population from 261,727 to 422,823 and Kentucky from 406,511 to 564,317. *Abstract of the Fourteenth Census*, 19.
2 *Journals of the General Conference*, I, 153-154.
3 *Ibid.*, I, 140, 142, 144, 160-161.
4 Tigert, *Constitutional History of Methodism*, 335.
5 *Journals of the General Conference*, I, 169-170.
6 McFerrin, *Methodism in Tennessee*, II, 413.

largely caused by the division of the region within the limits of the Tennessee Conference. The work of this area was conducted by fifty-two preachers,[7] one of whom was Benjamin Odgen, who was readmitted thirty years after his defection from the church.[8] The roster of presiding elders included the names of men of ability. Salt River was given to Marcus Lindsey; Nashville, to Thomas L. Douglass; Cumberland, to John McGee; Green River, to James Axley; Holston, to Jesse Cunningham; and French Broad, to John Henninger.[9]

As the Southwest emerged from the financial stringency dating from the War of 1812, the people, with a widened outlook, turned to some of the happier conditions of living. The mode of living was more comfortable; the chinked log cabin had been discarded for a better house. The church was now faced with the problems which grew out of a more complex society. The old reliable camp meeting had lost its popularity, and to many of the prospective church members the approach had to be made in a different manner. Slavery had slowly filtered into the life of the states, and the Methodist Church recognized that it was a weak church financially, and that it chiefly attracted the poorer class.[10] A low rumbling of dissatisfaction was heard among some of the leaders because they were unable to secure the membership of slave owners.[11] Church regulations and restrictions on slaveholding were modified again and again. The church founders never would have recognized the terms of admission which now permitted the planter and slaveholder to join the church.

To what extent the presence of the slave owner in the church militated against the poor people is a question that cannot be answered satisfactorily. Evidently they were able to work in some degree of accord. In the more remote sections the new

---

7 *Minutes*, I, 295-298.
8 Finley, *Sketches*, 48; Redford, *Methodism in Kentucky*, II, 385-389.
9 *Minutes*, I, 298.
10 McAnally, *Life and Times of Patton*, 100, 184; G. G. Smith, *The Life and Times of George Foster Pierce* (Sparta, Georgia, 1888), 561.
11 The changed attitude toward wealth may clearly be seen by reference to an early *Discipline*, for example that of 1812, page 181. Price contended that the slave rule drew to the Methodist Church the poorer classes of people and drove the wealthy and more influential ones into the Episcopal and Presbyterian churches. Price, *Holston Methodism*, II, 244. This statement could hardly be true after 1824 in the light of the slavery regulation of that year.

element of wealth made little difference. Then, as now, there was a separation of church-goers, each clinging to his own social level.

By 1824 the church had grown wealthier and was providing new and better buildings for its services.[12] The internal effect of a wealthy membership was detected by Thomas L. Douglass on his return visit to Tennessee in 1824. Here he found the appearance of the Methodist preacher greatly changed from the former neat and simple dress. Jewelry was now being worn by the women, and it was impossible to hold down the fashion of the day.[13] During this period Peter Cartwright was thundering away against sinful expenditures. "Look," said he, "at the ornamented pulpits, pewed and cushioned seats, organs, and almost all kinds of instruments, with salaried choirs and as proud and graceless as a fallen ghost . . . . "[14] Liberality of opinion and laxity in discipline were everywhere prevalent.[15]

The church now had within itself the potentialities of an extensive program of expansion. Methodism began extending its appointments into newer sections and fields. In 1815 the first circuit was laid out in the Territory of Arkansas and was given to the care of the Missouri District. Within that year Eli Lindsay reported ninety-two members in the Spring River Circuit.[16] In the summer of 1820 a meeting house was built in Montgomery, Alabama. Montgomery had been a thriving town long before any effort was made to erect a church there. As early as 1822 it boasted that the "mercantile business done here far exceeds that of any town of the same magnitude we have ever known."[17] While the Mississippi Conference was in session at Washington, Mississippi, in 1821, a new appointment was made which provided that Alexander Talley was to go to Pensacola, Mobile, Blakely, and the adjoining country.[18] New Orleans had no pastoral charge from 1815 to 1820, because there was no fund to support a missionary, and other sections could be occupied to a better

---
12 Cartwright, *Autobiography*, 234-235.
13 Brooks, *Life and Times*, 14.
14 Cartwright, *Autobiography*, 235.
15 McAnally, *Life and Times of Patton*, 114.
16 Jewell, *Methodism in Arkansas*, 29; *Minutes*, I, 280.
17 West, *Methodism in Alabama*, 348, 349.
18 *Minutes*, I, 387; West, *Methodism in Alabama*, 249.

advantage.[19] New Orleans appeared, however, in the *Minutes* of 1819, and thereafter the Methodist Church held its ground there in face of "a pleasure-loving dissolute, heterogeneous population" that "was divided between superstition and infidelity."[20]

In the face of extensive missionary plans membership statistics of the Tennessee and Mississippi conferences in 1818 indicate a very meager gain over the previous year.[21] This standstill, however, did not mean that a point of saturation had been reached, for not all of those eligible were already members of a church. Tennessee lagged in population because of the new lands which had been opened for settlement, and because of the wanderlust which called to the pioneer.[22] The land hungry population in a section already filled was unwilling to let broad fertile acres in the North, South, or West slip from its grasp.[23] Land mania had seized the people, and the newer sections were sought by a never ending stream of immigrants.[24] It has been said "that it seemed as if Virginia, Carolina, Kentucky, and Tennessee had agreed to pour out their citizens into Missouri and Illinois for the purpose of making them states. In his quest of new land the early Western man in spite of his gross nature became an idealist."[25] "Some who had come too late to get space there or who had lost their substance through extravagant living or misfortune trekked again across the Ohio, or boated to Missouri or Mississippi, seeking a new rainbow's end . . . ."[26]

Following a people who sought a new Eldorado, the Methodist Church further extended itself in the formation of the Kentucky Conference from that portion of Kentucky lying northwest of the Green River, which had been included in the Ohio Conference, and the Green, Salt, and Cumberland districts, which

---

19 Jones, *Methodism in Mississippi*, I, 369; McTyeire, *History of Methodism*, 546-550.
20 *Ibid.*, 548. See, also, Albert Phelps, *Louisiana: A Record of Expansion* (New York, 1905), 207-214; Lyle Saxon, *Old Louisiana* (New York, 1929), ch. ix, "The City of Sin"; Saxon, *Fabulous New Orleans* (New York, 1928), *passim*.
21 See *Minutes*, I, 310, 328, 329.
22 For a list of Indian treaties that affected Tennessee see A. C. Holt, "The Economic and Social Beginnings of Tennessee," *Tenn. Hist. Mag.*, VII (1921-1923), 226-227.
23 P. J. Treat, *The National Land System* (New York, 1910), 104.
24 McMaster, *History of the United States*, IV, 381-388.
25 See F. J. Turner, "The Problem of the West," *Atlantic Monthly*, LXXVIII (1896), 289-297.
26 U. B. Phillips, *Life and Labor in the Old South* (Boston, 1929), 84.

METHODISM REACHES MATURITY 127

previously belonged to the Tennessee Conference.[27] A combined report of the Tennessee and Kentucky conferences in 1821 shows that together they furnished over eleven thousand of the twenty-one thousand members gained during the year 1820-1821.[28]

With the growth of the Western country both in extent and population, the growth of the Methodist Episcopal Church had been commensurate. Frequent reshifting of territory was necessary to provide for the best work of the church. The General Conference of 1824 realized that the territory within Tennessee was too thickly peopled to be adequately cared for by the one conference. So the Tennessee was divided into two conferences, the Holston and the Tennessee. The latter was to include all of Tennessee south of the Cumberland River and west of the Cumberland Mountains, and that part of Alabama north of the watershed between Mobile Bay and the Tennessee River. The Holston was to include the remaining portion of Tennessee, and the sections of Virginia and North Carolina which were embraced in the Holston District, together with the Black Mountain and the French Broad circuits from the South Carolina Conference. The scope of the church had also grown beyond the jurisdiction of three bishops. At least two more were needed to serve the continent, and after much discussion and three ballots, Joshua Soule and Elijah Hedding were elected bishops.[29]

Starting from the Baltimore nucleus in 1784 Methodism within forty years covered the entire Middle West. Members had been added at the rapid average of eight thousand a year from 1784 to 1824, and the total membership had increased from eighteen thousand to over 341,000. The number of preachers had grown from 104 to 1,314. Exactly the same number of preachers were now serving the Holston and Tennessee conferences as at the beginning had ministered to the whole of the church in America. The seed of Western Methodism had been given to Jeremiah Lambert's care on the Holston Circuit where Virginia and Tennessee meet; in full growth it now flourished over all

---
[27] *Journals of the General Conference*, I, 216. This change was made at the General Conference held in 1816 at Baltimore.
[28] *Minutes*, I, 346, 366.
[29] *Journals of the General Conference*, I, 274-275, 285.

the settled regions of the Mississippi Valley. As the population had shifted from one fertile section to another, so Methodism had moved. The preacher had shared the fate and fortune of all out-post settlers; he had sprung from their ranks, and knew as no outlander could have ever known the needs and emergencies of his duty. He served as the connecting link between the backwoods and the Piedmont. At annual and general conferences, he learned news of concern to his circuit—of relatives, friends, political events, and foreign relations. In time he transferred the meager literary products from the publishing house to the frontier reader. Through his leadership schools were provided for the children to attend on both Sundays and week-days. As an active agent of reform the preacher fought immorality and intemperance, and attempted to stamp out in the Westerner that intense disregard for law. His manifold contributions to society were but as a background for his real duty. He had come to that section to convince the people of their sins, their need for salvation, and to reveal the new life which came from church membership. To this end he preached a religion, the doctrine of which suited the Western mind and the unsteady state of Western morals.

The preacher worked as an agent for a church organization that was flexible to the needs of Western society. As new fields opened up the mechanics of Methodism were adjusted to the fresh endeavors. The one Western Conference was increased to seven; its two districts in 1795 were twenty-eight in 1824; its seven circuits were now over two hundred, extending from the Great Lakes to the Gulf and as far west as St. Louis and Hot Springs; the membership had increased from 2,400 to 114,000; its twelve preachers, who had followed the mountain paths and trekked the dusty roads, had increased to nearly four hundred[30] who had "helped to make the sour-mud-swamp and the bristling brier patch into the fruitful meadow of today."[31]

---

30 *Minutes*, I, 24, 69, 70, 449-473. The dates on which the thirteen annual conferences met ranged from September 2, 1824 to September 14, 1825. The conference years varied accordingly, but the statistics read "Minutes for 1825." Thus the figures cannot be specified as exactly indicating the calendar year of 1824.

31 Extract from an eulogy by Fletcher Wharton quoted by I. F. King, "Introduction of Methodism into Ohio," Ohio Arch. and Hist. Soc. *Publications*, X (1901-1902), 217.

Thus with the growth of the Old Southwest had come the growth of the Methodist Church through the religious activity for which it had shown such wise prescience and heroic devotion.

BIBLIOGRAPHY

PRIMARY MATERIALS

Manuscripts

Butler, M., *Manners and Habits of the Western Pioneer.* Durrett Collection, University of Chicago.

Lyle, John, *Diary of the Rev. John Lyle,* 1801-1803. Durrett Collection.

McAfee, Robert B., *Life and Times of Robert B. McAfee and His Family Connections.* Durrett Collection.

Printed Sources

"A Bill of Mortality," *Christian Instructor,* I (1824), 91-92.

Abstract of the Fourteenth Census of the United States. Washington, 1923.

Armenius, Theophilus [Thomas S. Hinde], "Account of the Rise and Progress of the Work of God in the Western Country," *Methodist Magazine,* II (1819), 221-224.

Asbury, Francis, *The Journal of Rev. Francis Asbury.* 3 vols., New York, 1852.

Beggs, S. R., *Pages from the Early History of the West and Northwest.* Cincinnati, 1868.

Bishop, Robert H., *An Outline History of the Church in the State of Kentucky.* Lexington, 1824.

Brackenridge, H. M., *History of the Western Insurrection in Western Pennsylvania.* Pittsburg, 1859.

Bradbury, John, *Travels in the Interior of America in the Years* 1809, 1810, 1811 (Thwaites, *Early Western Travels,* V, Cleveland, 1904).

Breazeale, J. W. M., *Life As It Is, or, Matters and Things in General.* Knoxville, 1842.

Brooks, John, *The Life and Times of the Rev. John Brooks Written by Himself.* Nashville, 1848.

Brunson, Alfred, *A Western Pioneer: or, Incidents of the Life and Time of Rev. Alfred Brunson.* 2 vols., New York, 1872-1879.

Burke, William, *Autobiography* (Finley, *Sketches of Western Methodism*). Cincinnati, 1857.

Carr, John, *Early Times in Middle Tennessee.* Nashville, 1857.

Cartwright, Peter, *Autobiography of Peter Cartwright the Backwoods Preacher.* Edited by W. P. Strickland. New York, 1857.

Fifty Years As a Presiding Elder. New York, 1871.

Carvossa, William (ed.), *A Memoir of Mr. William Carvossa—Sixty Years a Class-Leader in the Wesleyan Methodist Connection.* Nashville, 1873.

"Cherokee Mission," *Methodist Magazine,* IX (1826), 35-36.

Claiborne, J. F. H., *Life and Correspondence of John A. Quitman.* 2 vols., New York, 1860.

"Colleges and Academies," *Holston Messenger*, III (1828), 206-209.
"Commencement of the Great Revival of Religion in Kentucky and Tennessee in 1799" (a letter from John McGee to Thomas L. Douglass), *Methodist Magazine*, IV (1821), 189-191.
"Creek Indian Missions," *Methodist Magazine*, VI (1823), 476.
Doctrines and Disciplines of the Methodist Episcopal Church. Various editions.
Dow, Lorenzo, *History of Cosmopolite; or the Writings of Rev. Lorenzo Dow.* Cincinnati, 1858.
The Dealings of God, Man, and Devil, As Exemplified in the Life, Experiences, and Travels of Lorenzo Dow. Cincinnati, 1858.
Drake, Daniel, *Pioneer Life in Kentucky. A Series of Reminiscential Letters from Daniel Drake to his Children.* Cincinnati, 1870.
Eggleston, Edward, *The Circuit Rider: A Tale of the Heroic Age.* New York, 1893.
Emory, John (ed.), *The Works of the Reverend John Wesley.* 7 vols., New York, 1835.
"Extract from the Report of Committee on Missions," *Methodist Magazine*, VII (1824), 276-278.
"Fifth Anniversary of the Missionary Society of the Methodist Episcopal Church," *Methodist Magazine*, VII (1824), 232-234.
Finley, James B., *Autobiography of Rev. James B. Finley, or, Pioneer Life in the West.* Edited by W. P. Strickland. Cincinnati, 1854.
History of the Wyandot Mission at Upper Sandusky, Ohio, under the Direction of the Methodist Episcopal Church. Cincinnati, 1840.
Life Among the Indians. Cincinnati, n. d.
Sketches of Western Methodism: Biographical, Historical and Miscellaneous. Edited by W. P. Strickland. Cincinnati, 1857.
Flint, James, *Letters from America Containing Observations on the Climate and Agriculture of the Western States* (Thwaites, *Early Western Travels*, IX, Cleveland, 1904).
Flint, Timothy, *Recollections of the Last Ten Years Passed in Occasional Residences and Journeyings in the Valley of the Mississippi.* Boston, 1826.
The History and Geography of the Mississippi Valley. 2 vols., Cincinnati, 1832.
Fordham, Elias P., *Personal Narrative of Travels in Virginia, Maryland, Pennsylvania, Ohio, Indiana, Kentucky; and of a Residence in the Illinois Territory: 1817-1818.* Edited by F. A. Ogg. Cleveland, 1906.
"Fourth Anniversary of the Missionary Society of the Methodist Episcopal Church," *Methodist Magazine*, VI (1823), 275-279.
Gaddis, Maxwell P., *Foot-Prints of an Itinerant.* Cincinnati, 1874.
Last Words and Old-Time Memories. Cincinnati, 1880.

Gillies, John, *Memoirs of Rev. George Whitefield.* Middletown, Connecticut, 1829.
Green, William M., *Life and Papers of A. L. P. Green.* Nashville, 1887.
Hall, James, *Romance of Western History.* Cincinnati, 1857.
Sketches of History, Life and Manners in the West. 2 vols., Philadelphia, 1835.
Halsey, Le Roy J. (ed.), *The Works of Philip Lindsley,* D. D. 3 vols., Philadelphia, 1866.
Hamilton, Thomas, *Men and Manners in America.* London, 1843.
Harris, Corra, *A Circuit Rider's Wife.* Philadelphia, 1910.
Hart, Albert B. (ed.), *National Expansion,* 1783-1845. New York, 1901.
Hinde, Thomas S., "Recollections of Mrs. Mary Todd Hinde," *Methodist Magazine,* XIII (1831), 121-132.
Impartial Review, Nashville, 1806.
Jefferson, Thomas, *Notes on the State of Virginia.* Philadelphia, 1794.
Journals of the General Conference of the Methodist Episcopal Church, 1796-1836. New York, 1855.
Journals of the Ohio Annual Conference, 1812-1826 (Sweet, *Circuit-Rider Days Along the Ohio,* 99-292).
Journal of the Western Conference, 1800-1811 (Sweet, *The Rise of Methodism in the West,* 73-207).
Knoxville Gazette, 1791-1796.
"Learned Ministers," *Holston Messenger,* III (1828), 209-213.
Lee, Jessie, *A Short History of the Methodists in the United States of America: Beginning in 1766, and Continued Till 1809.* Boston, 1810.
"Letter to a Junior Preacher," *Methodist Magazine,* VII (1824), 111-114.
Lyell, Charles, *A Second Visit to the United States.* 2 vols., London, 1849.
McNemar, Richard, *The Kentucky Revival.* Cincinnati, 1807.
"Memoir of Robert Raikes, Esq.," *Methodist Magazine,* XI (1828), 293-302.
Methodist Magazine (London), 1803-1827.
Methodist Magazine (New York), I-XX, 1818-1838.
"Methodist Missions Among the Cherokees," *Methodist Magazine* (London), 1827, p. 338.
Milburn, William H., *Ten Years of Preacher Life.* New York, 1859.
The Pioneers, Preachers, and People of the Mississippi Valley. New York, 1860.
The Rifle, Axe, and Saddle Bags. New York, 1857.
Minutes of the Annual Conferences of the Methodist Episcopal Church for the Years 1773-1828. New York, 1840.
Minutes of the Indiana Conference, 1832-1844 (Sweet, *Circuit-Rider Days in Indiana,* 90-333).
Monette, John W., *History of the Discovery and Settlement of the Valley*

BIBLIOGRAPHY 133

of the Mississippi. 2 vols., New York, 1846.

Niles Register (Baltimore), V, 1814.

Nuttall, Thomas, Journal of Travels into the Arkansa Territory During the Year 1819 (Thwaites, Early Western Travels, XIII, Cleveland, 1904).

Olmsted, Frederick L., A Journey in the Seaboard Slave States. New York, 1856.

Paschall, Edwin, Old Times; or, Tennessee History for Tennessee Boys and Girls. Nashville, 1869.

Phillips, Ulrich B., and John R. Commons (eds.), A Documentary History of American Industrial Society. 10 vols., Cleveland, 1910.

Punshon, William M., Sermons. New York, 1860.

"Quadrennial Report of the Managers of the Missionary Society of the Methodist Episcopal Church," Methodist Magazine, VII (1824), 278-280.

Redford, A. H., Western Cavaliers: Embracing the History of the Methodist Episcopal Church in Kentucky from 1832-1844. Nashville, 1876.

"Report of the Committee on Education," Methodist Magazine, VII (1824), 276-277.

"Report of the Committee on Missions," Methodist Magazine, VII (1824), 277-278.

"Report of the Tennessee Conference Missionary Society," Methodist Magazine, VII (1824), 192-195.

"Review of Rev. H. B. Bascom's Inaugural Address," Methodist Magazine, XI (1828), 147-151.

Rogers, James R., The Cane Ridge Meeting House to which is Appended the Autobiography of B. W. Stone and a Sketch of David Purviance by William Rogers. Cincinnati, 1910.

Rogers, John, The Biography of Eld. Barton Warren Stone, Written by Himself: With Additions and Reflections by Elder John Rogers. Cincinnati, 1847.

"Sabbath Schools in the West," Holston Messenger, IV (1829), 27-29.

Scott, Edward, Laws of the State of Tennessee, including those of North Carolina now in Force in this State. 2 vols., Knoxville, 1821.

Smith, Joseph, Old Redstone: or Historical Sketches of Western Presbyterianism and its Early Ministers. Philadelphia, 1854.

Sullins, D., Recollections of an Old Man. Bristol, Tennessee, 1910.

"Sunday Schools," Holston Messenger, III (1828), 77.

Taylor, John, A History of Ten Baptist Churches of Which the Author Has Been Alternately a Member. Frankfort, Kentucky, 1823.

The Methodist Pocket Hymn-Book Revised and Improved Designed as a Constant Companion for the Pious of All Denominations. New York, 1813.

"The Sunday School Union of the Methodist Episcopal Church," *Methodist Magazine*, XI (1828), 349-353.

Tipple, Ezra S. (ed.), *The Heart of Asbury's Journal*. Cincinnati, 1904.

Treaties between the United States of America and the Several Indian Tribes from 1778-1837. Washington, 1837.

Watson, J. V., *Tales and Takings. Sketches and Incidents*. New York, 1856.

Weld, Isaac, *Travels Through the States of North America and the Provinces of Upper and Lower Canada During the Years 1795, 1796, and 1797*. London, 1799.

Wesley, John, *The Journal*. 4 vols., New York, 1907.

The Works of the Rev. John Wesley, A. M., Sometime Fellow of Lincoln College, Oxford. 14 vols., London, 1831.

"Wesley's Rules for Congregational Singing," *Methodist Magazine*, VII (1824), 189-190.

Whitefield, George, *The Works of the Reverend George Whitefield*. 2 vols., London, 1771-1772.

Williams, Joseph S., *Old Times in Tennessee. Reminiscences—Semi-historic—of Pioneer Life and the Early Emigrant Settlers in the Big Hatchie Country*. Memphis, 1873.

Williams, Samuel C. (ed.), *Early Travels in the Tennessee Country, 1540-1800*. Johnson City, Tennessee, 1928.

Young, Jacob, *Autobiography of a Pioneer; or the Nativity, Experience, Travels, and Ministerial Labors of Rev. Jacob Young*. Cincinnati, 1857.

SECONDARY MATERIALS

Abernethy, Thomas P., *From Frontier to Plantation in Tennessee*. Chapel Hill, 1932.

Adams, Charles, "Wesley, the Catholic," *Methodist Review* (New York, 1851), XXXIII, 177-198.

Adams, Henry, *History of the United States during the Administrations of Jefferson and Madison*. 9 vols., New York, 1889-1891.

Adams, James T., *The Epic of America*. Boston, 1931.

"A Fragment," *Christian Instructor*, I (1825), 156-157.

Alden, G. H., "The State of Franklin," *American Historical Review*, VIII (1902-1903), 271-289.

Alexander, James W., "The Sunday School in its Relation to the Church," *Methodist Review* (Nashville, 1890), IX, 520-521.

Allen, William B., *A History of Kentucky Embracing Gleanings, Reminiscences, Antiquities, Natural Curiosities, Statistics, and Biographical Sketches*. Louisville, 1872.

BIBLIOGRAPHY

Anderson, John M., "The Heroes of the Ministry in the Early History of Tennessee Methodism," *Tennessee Conference Journal*, 1912, pp. 103-116.

Anderson, Josephus, "Probationary Church Membership," *Methodist Review* (Nashville, 1858), XII, 535-543.

Andrews, James O., "Bishop Asbury," *Methodist Review* (Nashville, 1859), XIII, 1-11.
"Bishop McKendree," *Methodist Review* (Nashville, 1859), XIII, 161-170.

Archibald, F. A. (ed.), *Methodism and Literature: A Series of Articles from Several Writers on the Literary Enterprises and Achievements of the Methodist Episcopal Church.* New York, 1883.

Armenius, Theophilus [Thomas S. Hinde], "A Descriptive View of the Western Country," *Methodist Magazine*, VII (1824), 384-389.

Asbury, Herbert, "The Father of Prohibition," *American Mercury*, IX (1926), 344-348.

Ayers, Samuel G., "Francis Asbury and his Presbyterian Friends," *Methodist Review* (Nashville, 1917), LXVI, 467-475.

Babcock, Kendric C., *The Rise of American Nationality.* New York, 1906.

Bacon, L. W., *A History of American Christianity.* New York, 1897.

Ballagh, James C., *A History of Slavery in Virginia.* Baltimore, 1902.

Bancroft, George, *History of the United States of America.* 6 vols., New York, 1888.

Bangs, Nathan, *History of the Methodist Episcopal Church.* 4 vols., New York, 1857.

Barnes, Annie M., *Scenes in Pioneer Methodism.* 2 vols., Nashville, 1892.

Bennett, William W., *Memorials of Methodism in Virginia from Its Introduction into the State, in the Year 1772, to the Year 1829.* Richmond, 1871.
"Pioneer Methodism in Virginia," *Methodist Review* (Nashville, 1888), V, 79-98.

Berry, Joseph F., "The Methodist Episcopacy," *Christian Advocate*, CI (1926), 1128-1131.

Boswell, John W., *A Short History of Methodism.* Nashville, 1901.

Brown, Arlo A., "The Sunday School Movement—A Century of Development," *Christian Advocate*, CI (1926), 1155-1156.

Brown, Charles R., *The Larger Faith.* Boston, 1923.

Buckley, J. M., *A History of Methodists in the United States.* New York, 1896.
History of Methodism. 2 vols., New York, 1898.

Burrows, J. H., "History of Giles County," undated newspaper clipping in Tennessee State Library.

Caldwell, John H., "The Relations of the Colored People to the Methodist Episcopal Church, South," *Methodist Review* (Nashville, 1866), XLVIII, 418-435.
Candler, Warren A., *Great Revivals and the Great Republic.* Nashville, 1904.
Carroll, H. K., *Francis Asbury in the Making of American Methodism.* New York, 1923.
Channing, Edward, *A History of the United States.* 7 vols., New York, 1907-1932.
Chreitzberg, A. M., *Early Methodism in the Carolinas.* Nashville, 1897.
Christian, John T., *A History of the Baptists in Louisiana.* Shreveport, 1923.
Clark, J. O. A., "Methodism—Modern Sunday Schools," *Methodist Review* (Nashville, 1884), VI, 619-634.
"Class Meetings," *Holston Messenger,* III (1828), 81-82.
"Class Meetings," *Methodist Review* (Nashville, 1849), III, 574-603.
"Class Meetings," *Methodist Review* (Nashville, 1858), XII, 507-535.
Clayton, W. W., *History of Davidson County, Tennessee.* Philadelphia, 1880.
Cleveland, Catherine C., *The Great Revival in the West,* 1797-1805. Chicago, 1916.
Coggeshall, S. W., "A Review of the Rise and Progress of American Methodism," *Methodist Magazine,* XX (1838), 265-285.
Collins, Lewis, *History of Kentucky.* Louisville, 1877.
Conner, William F., "The Book Committee—What It Is and Does," *Christian Advocate,* CI (1926), 1180-1182.
Conoly, W. J., "The Catholicity of Methodism," *Methodist Review* (Nashville, 1916), LXV, 716-728.
Cook, J. F., *Old Kentucky.* New York, 1908.
Corderay, Edward, *Father Reeves, The Model Class Leader.* Nashville, 1854.
Cossitt, F. R., *The Life and Times of Rev. Finis Ewing.* Louisville, 1857.
Cotterill, R. S., *History of Pioneer Kentucky.* Cincinnati, 1917.
Cummings, A. W., *The Early Schools of Methodism.* New York, 1886.
Cutshall, Elmer G., *The Doctrinal Training of the Travelling Ministry of the Methodist Episcopal Church of the United States.* Ph. D. thesis, University of Chicago, 1922.
Davenport, Frederick M., *Primitive Traits in Religious Revivals.* New York, 1905.
Davidson, Robert, *History of the Presbyterian Church in the State of Kentucky.* New York, 1847.
Davis, Lyman E., "The Methodist Protestant Church," *Christian Advocate,* CI (1926), 1135-1136.

Dean, Kenneth W., *Social and Economic Conditions in Kentucky As Reflected in the Newspapers, 1788-1804.* M. A. thesis, University of Chicago, 1925.

Downey, David G., "The Fountain of Books," *Christian Advocate,* CI (1926), 1182-1183.

Drew, Samuel, *The Life of the Rev. Thomas Coke, D. D.* New York, 1837.

Driver, Carl S., *John Sevier, Pioneer of the Old Southwest.* Chapel Hill, 1932.

The Effects of their Environment on the Social, Educational, and Religious Practices of the German Baptist Brethren. M. A. thesis, Vanderbilt University, 1924.

Du Bose, Horace M., *Francis Asbury, A Biographical Study.* Nashville, 1916.

Duncan, Fannie C., *When Kentucky Was Young.* Louisville, 1928.

Duvall, S. T., *The Methodist Episcopal Church and Education Up to 1869.* New York, 1928.

Eddy, T. M., "Influence of Methodism Upon the Civilization and Education of the West," *Methodist Review* (New York, 1857), XXXIX, 280-296.

"Education in the Methodist Episcopal Church, South," *Methodist Review* (Nashville, 1859), XIII, 12-27.

Edwards, John E., *Life of Rev. John Wesley Childs.* Louisville, 1852.

Emory, Robert, *The Life of Rev. John Emory.* New York, 1841.

Faulkner, John A., *The Methodists.* New York, 1903.

Fitzgerald, O. P., *Centenary Cameos.* Nashville, 1885.

John B. McFerrin. Nashville, 1888.

The Class Meeting. Nashville, 1898.

Frazier, J. Tyler, "The Old Time Circuit Rider: His Place and Influence in Tennessee Methodism," *Tennessee Conference Journal,* 1912, pp. 128-132.

Frost, W. G., "Our Contemporary Ancestors in the Southern Mountains," *Atlantic Monthly,* LXXXIII (1899), 311-319.

Fry, B. St. James, "The Early Camp Meeting Song Writers," *Methodist Review* (New York, 1859), XLI, 401-413.

Fuller, Myron L., "Our Greatest Earthquakes," *Popular Science Monthly,* LXIX (1916), 76-82.

"The New Madrid Earthquake," *U. S. Geological Survey Bulletin,* 1912, no. 404.

Galloway, C. B., "Thomas Griffin: A Boanerges of the Early Southwest," Mississippi Historical Society *Publications,* VII (1903), 153-170.

Gewehr, W. M., "Some Factors in the Expansion of Frontier Methodism, 1800-1811," *Journal of Religion,* VIII (1928), 98-120.

Gilmore, W. E., *Life of Edward Tiffin, First Governor of Ohio.* Chillicothe, 1897.

Grissom, W. L., *History of Methodism in North Carolina*. Nashville, 1905.

Grose, George R., "The Gospel of John Wesley, With Some Reflections Upon the Preaching for the Times," *Methodist Review* (New York, 1912), XCIV, 271-282.

Hale, W. T. and D. L. Merritt, *A History of Tennessee and Tennesseans*. 8 vols., Chicago, 1913.

Hall, Mitchell, *Johnson County Kentucky, A History of the County, and Genealogy of Its People up to the Year 1927*. 2 vols., Louisville, 1928.

Hamilton, W., "Early Methodism in Maryland, Especially in Baltimore," *Methodist Review* (New York, 1856), XXXVIII, 431-448.

Harper, Earl E., "The Music and Worship of Methodism," *Christian Advocate*, CI (1926), 1138-1139.

Hart, Albert B., *Slavery and Abolition*. New York, 1906.

Henderson, Archibald, *Conquest of the Old Southwest*. New York, 1920.

Hendrix, E. R., "The Evolution of the Methodist Hymnal," *Methodist Review* (Nashville, 1906), LV, 3-18.

"The General Conference of 1808," *Methodist Review* (Nashville, 1908), LVII, 692-711.

Henkle, Moses M., *Primary Platforms of Methodism or Exposition of the General Rules*. Louisville, 1851.

The Life of Henry Bidleman Bascom. Nashville, 1860.

Hill, Felix R., "Heroes Among the Laity in the Early History of Tennessee Methodism," *Tennessee Conference Journal*, 1912, pp. 117-127.

"History of Methodist Missions," *Methodist Magazine*, XIV (1832), 249-254.

Holt, Albert C., "The Economic and Social Beginnings of Tennessee," *Tennessee Historical Magazine*, VII (1921-1922), 194-230, 252-313; VIII (1924), 24-80.

Hoss, E. E., "Bishop William McKendree," *Methodist Review* (Nashville, 1915), LXIV, 40-74.

David Morton: A Biography. Nashville, 1916.

"Elihu Embree, Abolitionist," *American Historical Magazine* (Nashville, 1897), II, 113-138.

"Impure Air in Churches," *Methodist Magazine*, IX (1826), 102-103.

James, William, *The Varieties of Religious Experience*. New York, 1922.

Jameson, J. Franklin, "The American Acta Sanctorum," *American Historical Review*, XIII (1907-1908), 286-302.

Jarrell, Charles C., *Methodism on the March*. Nashville, 1924.

Jewell, Horace, *History of Methodism in Arkansas*. Little Rock, 1892.

Jones, John G., *A Complete History of Methodism as Connected with the Mississippi Conference of the Methodist Episcopal Church, South*. 2 vols., Nashville, 1887.

Kelley, D. C., "Methodist Church Membership," *Methodist Review* (Nashville, 1884), VI, 45-49.

Kerley, T. A., *Conference Rights; or, Governing Principles.* Nashville, 1898.
"One Hundred Years of Missionary Operations in the Tennessee Conference," *Tennessee Conference Journal,* 1912, pp. 156-164.
King, I. F., "Introduction of Methodism into Ohio," Ohio Archeological and Historical Society *Publications,* X (1901-1902), 165-219.
Lecky, W. E. H., *History of European Morals.* 2 vols., London, 1911.
Levering, Julia H., *Historic Indiana.* New York, 1916.
Lovejoy, W. P., "The Influence of Methodism," *Methodist Review* (Nashville, 1902), LI, 367-382.
Luccock, H. E. and Paul Hutchinson, *The Story of Methodism.* Cincinnati, 1926.
MacDonald, William, *Jacksonian Democracy.* New York, 1906.
McAnally, D. R., *Life and Times of Rev. S. Patton and Annals of Holston Conference.* Saint Louis, 1859.
McClintock, John D., "The Sunday School in Its Relation to the Church," *Methodist Review* (Nashville, 1857), XI, 513-531.
McDonnold, B. W., *History of the Cumberland Presbyterian Church.* Nashville, 1899.
McFerrin, John B., *History of Methodism in Tennessee.* 3 vols., Nashville, 1871-1874.
McLean, J. P., "The Kentucky Revival and Its Influence on the Miami Valley," Ohio Archeological and Historical Society *Publications,* XIII (1903), 242-280.
McMaster, John B., *A History of the People of the United States.* 7 vols., New York, 1885-1892.
McSwain, W. A., "Philosophy of Methodist Itineracy," *Methodist Review* (Nashville, 1891), X, 120-130.
McTyeire, H. N., *A History of Methodism.* Nashville, 1884.
Mallard, Robert Q., *Plantation Life before Emancipation.* Richmond, 1892.
Martin, Asa Earl, *The Anti-Slavery Movement in Kentucky Prior to 1850.* Louisville, 1918.
"The Anti-Slavery Societies in Tennessee," *Tennessee Historical Magazine,* I, (1915), 261-281.
Matlack, Lucius C., "Our Past and Present Relations to Slavery," *Methodist Review* (New York, 1868), L, 252-263.
The Antislavery Struggle and Triumph in the Methodist Episcopal Church. New York, 1881.
The History of American Slavery and Methodism. New York, 1849.
Mellen, G. F., "Early Methodism and the Cherokees," *Methodist Review* (Nashville, 1917), LXVI, 476-487.
Mesick, Jane L., *The English Traveller in America.* New York, 1922.
Methodist Review (Nashville), III-LXXIV, 1849-1925.
Methodist Review (New York), XXXIII-XCIV, 1851-1912.

Mileham, Hazel B., *History of Higher Education of the Methodist Church in the United States from 1820-1844.* M. A. thesis, University of Chicago, 1926.

Miley, John, *Class Meetings.* Cincinnati, 1859.

"Ministerial Support," *Methodist Review* (Nashville, 1892), XII, 93-104.

Mode, Peter G., "Revivalism as a Phase of Frontier Life," *Journal of Religion,* I (1921), 337-354.
The Frontier Spirit in American Christianity. New York, 1923.

Moore, David H., "The Philosophy of Methodist 'Success," *Tennessee Conference Journal,* 1912, pp. 165-174.

Moore, M. H., *Sketches of the Pioneers in North Carolina and Virginia.* Nashville, 1884.

Neely, Thomas B., *Doctrinal Standards of Methodism.* Chicago, 1918.

Nelson, Wilbur A., "Reelfoot—An Earthquake Lake," *National Geographic Magazine,* XLV (1924), 95-110.

Nogler, Arthur W., *The Church in History.* Cincinnati, 1929.

Noll, Arthur H., *History of the Church in the Diocese of Tennessee.* New York, 1900.

North, Eric M., "A Study of the Divisions of American Methodism," *Christian Advocate,* CI (1926), 1132-1133.

North, Frank M., "The Foreign Missions of the Methodist Episcopal Church," *Christian Advocate,* CI (1926), 1147-1149.

Norwood, John H., *The Schism in the Methodist Episcopal Church 1844: A Study of Slavery and Ecclesiastical Politics.* New York, 1923.

Nowlin, William D., *Kentucky Baptist History, 1770-1922.* Baptist Book Concern, 1922.

"Old Methodism," *Methodist Magazine,* XIX (1837), 212-227.

"Origin of Sunday Schools," *Methodist Magazine,* IX (1826), 150-152.

Paine, Robert, *Life and Times of William McKendree.* Nashville, 1880.

Parrington, Vernon L., *The Colonial Mind,* 1620-1800. New York, 1927.

Paxson, Frederic L., *History of the American Frontier,* 1763-1893. Boston, 1924.

Peoples, R. G., "Secondary Education in the Tennessee Conference," *Tennessee Conference Journal,* 1912, pp. 133-138.

Perrin, W. H., J. H. Battle, G. C. Kniffen, *History of Kentucky.* Louisville, 1886.

"Peter Cartwright," *American Historical Record,* I (1872), 567.

Phelan, James, *History of Tennessee.* Boston, 1889.

Phelps, Albert, *Louisiana, A Record of Expansion.* New York, 1905.

Phillips, Ulrich B., *American Negro Slavery.* New York, 1918.
Life and Labor in the Old South. Boston, 1929.

Pickett, Albert J., *History of Alabama and Incidentally of Georgia and Mississippi from the Earliest Period.* Birmingham, 1900.

Pickett, Deets, "The Methodists and the Drink Traffic," *Christian Advocate*, CI (1926), 1221-1223, 1226, 1230.

Porter, James, "The Methodist Book Concern," *Methodist Review* (New York, 1867), XLIX, 267-287.

The Revised Compendium of Methodism. New York, 1875.

Prather, Charles H., "Francis Asbury, Apostle," *Methodist Review* (Nashville, 1916), LXV, 323-333.

Preston, Thomas W., *Historical Sketches of the Holston Valley.* Kingsport, Tennessee, 1926.

Price, Carl F., "A Century of Methodist Song," *Christian Advocate*, CI (1926), 1139-1141.

Price, R. N., *Holston Methodism from Its Origin to the Present Time.* 5 vols., Nashville, 1912-1913.

Provine, W. A., "Tennessee's Earliest Educational Institutions," *Tennessee Historical Magazine.* 2nd. series, vol. II (1932), 165-178.

"Publishers of the Christian Advocate, 1826-1926," *Christian Advocate*, CI (1926), 1108-1109.

Pusey, William A., *The Wilderness Road to Kentucky; Its Location and Features.* New York, 1921.

Putnam, A. W., *History of Middle Tennessee.* Nashville, 1859.

Ramsay, David, *The History of South Carolina from Its First Settlement in 1670 to the Year 1809.* 2 vols., Charleston, 1809.

Ramsey, J. G. M., *The Annals of Tennessee.* Philadelphia, 1860.

Ranck, George W., *Boonesborough.* Louisville, 1901.

Redford, A. H., *Life and Times of H. H. Kavanaugh.* Nashville, 1884.

The History of Methodism in Kentucky. 3 vols., Nashville, 1868-1870.

Riley, B. F., *History of the Baptists in Alabama.* Birmingham, 1895.

Rogers, James R., *The Cane Ridge Meeting House to which is Appended the Autobiography of B. W. Stone and a Sketch of David Purviance by William Rogers.* Cincinnati, 1910.

Roosevelt, Theodore, *Winning of the West.* 6 vols., New York, 1905.

Ross, E. A., *Social Psychology.* New York, 1914.

Rusk, Ralph L., *The Literature of the Middle Western Frontier.* 2 vols., New York, 1925.

Sampson, Frances A., "The New Madrid and Other Earthquakes in Missouri," *Proceedings of the Mississippi Valley Historical Association*, VI (1912-1913), 218-238.

Sassnett, W. J., "Theory of Methodist Class Meetings," *Methodist Review* (Nashville, 1851), V, 265-284.

"The Relation of the Church to Missions," *Methodist Review* (Nashville, 1852), VI, 250-279.

Saxon, Lyle, *Fabulous New Orleans.* New York, 1928.

Old Louisiana. New York, 1929.

Schlup, Emil, "The Wyandot Mission," Ohio Archeological and Historical Society *Publications,* XV (1906), 163-181.

Seaton, John L., "Methodism and Education," *Christian Advocate* CI (1926), 1153-1155.

Seldes, Gilbert, *The Stammering Century.* New York, 1928.

Sellers, Charles C., *Lorenzo Dow The Bearer of the Word.* New York, 1928.

Semple, Ellen C., *American History and Its Geographic Conditions.* New York, 1903.

Smith, George G., *History of Methodism in Georgia and Florida from 1785-1865.* Macon, Georgia, 1881.
Life and Labors of Francis Asbury. Nashville, 1896.
The Life and Times of George Foster Pierce. Sparta, Georgia, 1888.

Smith, Justin A., *A History of the Baptists in the Western States East of the Mississippi.* Philadelphia, 1896.

Smith, Z. F., *History of Kentucky.* Louisville, 1886.

Smoot, Thomas A., "Religious Life in the Old South," *Methodist Review* (Nashville, 1925), LXXIV, 466-475.

Soule, Joshua, "The Methodist Church and Slavery," *Methodist Review* (Nashville, 1908), LVII, 637-650.

Speer, William, *The Great Revival of* 1800. Philadelphia, 1872.

Spivey, Ludd M., *Methodist Education in America Prior to* 1820. M. A. thesis, University of Chicago, 1922.

Stevens, Abel, *History of American Methodism.* New York, 1867.
History of the Methodist Episcopal Church. 4 vols., New York, 1864-1867.
Life and Times of Nathan Bangs, D. D. New York, 1863.

Stevens, William B., *A History of Georgia from its Discovery by Europeans to the Adoption of the Present Constitution in* 1798. 2 vols., New York, 1847.

Sweet, William W., *Circuit-Rider Days in Indiana.* Indianapolis, 1916.
Circuit-Rider Days Along the Ohio. Cincinnati, 1920.
"The Coming of the Circuit Rider Across the Mountains," *Mississippi Valley Historical Review,* IX (1922-1923), 271-282.
The Methodist Episcopal Church and the Civil War. Cincinnati, 1912.
The Rise of Methodism in the West. Cincinnati, 1920.

Taylor, Oliver, *Historic Sullivan.* Bristol, Tennessee, 1909.

"The Christian Advocate," *Christian Advocate,* CI (1926), 1094-1095.

Tigert, John J., *A Constitutional History of American Episcopal Methodism.* Nashville, 1894.

Tillett, W. F., "Methodism and Higher Education in the Tennessee Conference," *Tennessee Conference Journal,* 1912, pp. 139-155.
"Methodist Hymnology," *Methodist Review* (Nashville, 1903), LII, 333-348.

BIBLIOGRAPHY 143

Tipple, Ezra S., *Francis Asbury, the Prophet of the Long Road.* New York, 1916.

"Methodism and Theological Education," *Christian Advocate,* CI (1926), 1156-1159.

Treat, Payson J., *The National Land System.* New York, 1910.

Turner, F. J., *The Frontier in American History.* New York, 1921.

"The Problem of the West," *Atlantic Monthly,* LXXVIII (1896), 289-297.

The Rise of the New West. New York, 1906.

"Western State Making in the Revolutionary Era," *American Historical Review,* I (1895-1896), 70-87, 251-269.

Tyerman, Luke, *Life and Times of John Wesley.* 3 vols., New York, 1872.

Tyler, B. B., *A History of the Disciples of Christ.* New York, 1894.

"Tyranny of Fashion," *Holston Messenger,* III (1828), 73-74.

Van Tyne, C. H., "Influence of the Clergy, and of Religious and Sectarian Forces, on the American Revolution," *American Historical Review,* XIX (1913-1914), 44-64.

Wardle, Addie G., *History of the Sunday School Movement in the Methodist Episcopal Church.* New York, 1918.

Weigle, Luther A., *American Idealism.* New Haven, 1928.

West, Anson, *A History of Methodism in Alabama.* Nashville, 1892.

Wheeler, Henry, *Methodism and the Temperance Reform.* New York, 1882.

"Relations of the Methodist Episcopal Church to the Cause of Temperance," *Methodist Review* (New York, 1876), LVIII, 628-643.

Whitaker, Arthur P., "The Muscle Shoals Speculation," *Mississippi Valley Historical Review,* XIII (1926-1927), 365-386.

The Spanish American Frontier: 1783-1795. New York, 1927.

White, Andrew D., *A History of the Warfare of Science with Theology in Christendom.* 2 vols., New York, 1925.

Whitlock, W. F., *The Story of the Book Concerns.* Cincinnati, 1903.

Wightman, William M., *The Life of William Capers, D. D.* Nashville, 1859.

Williams, Charles B., *A History of the Baptists in North Carolina.* Raleigh, 1901.

Williams, Samuel C., *Beginnings of West Tennessee,* 1541-1841. Johnson City, Tennessee, 1930.

Williams, Samuel W., *Pictures of Early Methodism in Ohio.* Cincinnati, 1909.

Williamson, Hugh, *The History of North Carolina.* 2 vols., Philadelphia, 1812.

Wilson, David, "Local Preachers," *Methodist Review* (Nashville, 1882), IV, 705-712.

Winchester, C. T., *The Life of John Wesley.* New York, 1921.

Woodward, Comer M., *Philanthropic Aspects of Early Methodism.* B. D. thesis, University of Chicago, 1917.
Wooldridge, John (ed.), *History of Nashville, Tennessee.* Nashville, 1890.
Wright, Richardson, *Hawkers and Walkers in Early America.* Philadelphia, 1927.

INDEX

Abolition societies, 93.
Acuff's Chapel, 6.
Adams, William, 59.
African Methodist Episcopal Church, 99.
Allen, Richard, 99.
Ament, Samuel, 76.
American Bible Society, 79.
American Sunday School Union, 75.
American Tract Society, 12.
Amos, Abraham, 64.
Annual conference, plan, 115.
Arkansas Territory, circuit formed, 125.
Arminian Magazine, 74.
Asbury, Francis, 96; bishop, 2; opposition to Wesley, 3; in West, 6; in Kentucky, 8; catches itch, 11; in Tennessee, 14; in Nashville, 18, 33; camp meetings, 20, 31; infirmities, 32; travels, 37, 61; herbal remedy, 40; reading list, 41; at Tennessee Conference, 55, 58; on War of 1812, 57, 58; on marriage, 59; at Ohio Conference, 60; death, 61; on education, 63; Sunday schools, 74; on slavery, 92; on whiskey, 101, 102; expels preachers, 109; council plan, 113.
Asbury Manual Labor School, 85.
Athens College, 72.
Augusta College, 68.
Augusta Herald, 80.
Axley, James, 36, 124; on whiskey, 104; sermon on intemperance, 107; on tobacco, 109; anecdote, 110.
Bancroft, George, 3.
Band, 109; purpose, 118.
Baptists, in Kentucky, 7; over-sight of negroes, 98.
Bascom, Henry B., 11; humorous incidents, 38; slavery attitude, 97; Madison Circuit, 115.
Beecher, Lyman, 11; on whiskey, 100, 102.
Bethel College, 70; subscriptions for, 8; sketch, 63.
Bethesda orphanage, 93.
Bishop, duties, 119; election, 120.
Blackbird, Joseph, 89.
Blackman, Learner, 32, 58, 59, 96.
Book Concern, Philadelphia, 78; publications, 79; Cincinnati, 80.
Borromeo, Cardinal, 73.
Bowman, E. W., 32, 44.
Boyd, Robert, 86.
Bracken Academy, 68.
Brunson, Alfred, 111.
Bryan, Eliza, 49.

INDEX

Burke, William, 15.
Burton, John, 91.
Camp meetings, psychology of, 18, 22; origin, 19; in Tennessee, 20; preparations for, 21; routine, 22; Cane Ridge, Kentucky, 22; preachers, 23, 28; sermons, 24; procedure, 24; emotional exercises, 24, 26, 27; Cabin Creek, Kentucky, 27; grossness, 29; immorality, 30; results, 31; Ebenezer, Tennessee, 60; Murfreesboro, Tennessee, 60; among Indians, 86; altar, 87; appeal to negroes, 98; whiskey, 103, 106.
Capers, William, sketch, 85; missionary to negroes, 98.
Cartwright, Peter, 34, 59, 105; enforces Discipline, 12; encounter with rowdies, 39, 106; on earthquakes, 52; on War of 1812, 57; on education, 65; on Cokesbury, 67; D. D., 72; intemperate preachers, 102; fashions, 118; expensive church, 125.
Cherokee Indians, removal to Arkansas, 89.
Cherokee mission, 86; Upper and Lower missions, 87; membership, 88.
Choctaw mission, 89.
Christian Advocate, 75, 80, 103.
Christian Instructor, 108.
Christmas Conference, 2.
Circuit system, advantages, 66.
Clark, Francis, 7.
Class leader, duties, 117.
Class meeting, 109; purpose, 117.
Coke, Thomas, 113; sent to America, 2; returns to Europe, 33; death, 60; founds college, 63.
Cokesbury College, 63; sketch, 66.
Cole, Leroy, 59.
Council plan, 113.
Crawford, Andrew J., 83, 86.
Creek mission, 85.
Crouch, Benjamin Q., 84.
Cunningham, Jesse, 124.
Davis, Arthur, 39.
Deacon, 120.
Dickens, John, 78.
Discipline, 114; of 1784, 67, 74, 119; of 1796, 75, 104; expurgated edition, 96.
Dixon, William, 59.
Doak, Samuel, 6.
Doctors of Divinity, 72.
Doctrine, 42, 122.
Douglass, Thomas L., 82, 83, 123, 124; on missionaries, 85; report on missions, 88; in Tennessee, 125.
Dow, Lorenzo, personal appearance, 28; in Alabama, 32; patent medicine, 40; earthquakes, 49.

Durham, Benjamin, 117.
Earthquakes, 49; destruction by, 50; theories of cause, 50; religious effect, 51.
Edney, Leven, 96.
Ellicott, Andrew, 100.
Embree, Thomas, 93.
Emory and Henry College, 72.
Emory College, 72.
Exhorter, 121.
Falling exercises, 26.
Fields, Turtle, 88.
Finley, James B., 46, 69; Wyandot mission, 81; on reform, 105.
Finley, John P., 69.
Flint, Timothy, 42.
Floyd, Moses, 32; suspended, 44.
Franklin, constitution of 1785, 13.
Frontiersman, self-reliant, 5, 49; irreligious, 10; illiterate, 65; intemperate, 100.
Garrett, Lewis, 83.
Garrettson, Freeborn, 92.
General Conference, of 1796, 14; of 1812, 53; of 1820, 68, 81, 82, 119; of 1824, 88, 127; of 1780, 1796, 1812, 104; of 1816, 105, 123; origin, 113; plan, 114.
George, Enoch, 123.
Gibson, Tobias, 9.
Grant, Ulysses Simpson, 1.
Green, A. L. P., 40.
Grundy, Felix, 76.
Hamilton, Alexander, 103.
Harrison, William H., 84.
Harvard, 62.
Haw, James, 7, 8.
Hearn, Jacob, 83.
Hedding, Elijah, 127.
Henderson, Richard, 4, 19.
Henninger, John, 124.
Holland, Hezekiah, 82.
Holston Circuit, formed, 6.
Holston Conference, formed, 127.
Holston Messenger, 72, 80, 119.
Holy laugh, 24.
Hymns, 25, 42.
Indiana Territory, 102.
Indians, Wyandot mission, 81; missions in Jackson's Purchase, 82; Creek mission, 85; Cherokee mission, 85; Choctaw mission, 89.

Itinerant system, 35; advantage, 10; suitability to West, 13; size of circuits, 37.
Jackson's Purchase, 82; Indian mission, 82; church membership, 84.
Jefferson, Thomas, 100.
Jerks, 27.
Kentucky, settlement, 4; church membership, 16, 49.
Kentucky Circuit, formed, 7.
Kentucky Conference, of 1790, 8; of 1820, 82, 126; of 1824, 84.
Knoxville Gazette, 12, 93.
Knoxville, Tennessee, 103.
La Grange College, 72.
Lambert, Jeremiah, 6, 127.
Lindsay, Eli, 125.
Lindsey, Marcus, 34, 81, 124.
Lindsley, Philip, 100, 109.
Liquors, church rules, 103.
Local preacher, duties, 121.
Lotspiech, Ralph, 64.
Love feast, 119.
Lyle, John, 42.
McElroy, Archibald, 106.
McFerrin, John B., among Cherokees, 37; circuit, 89.
McGee, John, 20, 83, 124.
McGee, William, 20.
McGready, James, 19.
McKendree, William, advent in West, 17; bishop, 33; at Tennessee Conference, 55, 58, 123; injured, 58; at Ohio Conference, 58, 60; on marriage, 59; on tobacco, 111; with O'Kelly, 114; first presiding elder, 119; presiding elder contest, 119; despot, 120.
McKendree Church, 76.
McMahon, William, 86.
McNabb, Alexander, 112.
Maddin, Thomas, 77.
"Manumission Society of Tennessee," 94.
Meetinghouses, 38, 125.
Membership, admission, 121.
Methodist Magazine, 80.
Methodist Protestant Church, 120.
Methodist Publishing House, Nashville, 70.
Methodist Review, 80.
Milburn, William H., 43, 89.
Mills, Samuel, 79.
Ministerial education, 62; meager, 64; attitude toward, 64, 66, 68, 72; provisions for, 67, 71, 123.
Ministry, orders of, 120.

Missionary Society, organized, 81; report of 1824, 88.
Missions, to Indians, 81, 82, 85, 86, 89; to negroes, 98.
Mississippi Conference, 71; formed, 123; of 1821, 125.
Mississippi Territory, establishment of Methodism, 9.
Mississippi Valley, fertility, 48.
Montgomery, Alabama, 125.
Nashville, Tennessee, 9, 18, 33; Sunday school, 76.
Neeley, Richard, 85, 87.
Negroes, church over -sight, 97; appeal of camp meeting, 98; membership, 98.
New Orleans, Louisiana, 125.
O'Cull, James, 106.
Ogden, Benjamin, 7, 8; missionary to Indians, 84; readmitted, 124.
Ohio, establishment of Methodism, 9.
Ohio Conference, formed, 53, 123; of 1812, 56; of 1813, 58; of 1815, 60; Wyandot mission, 81.
O'Kelly, James, 14; schism, 113.
Osborn, Charles, 94.
Overall, Abraham, 83.
Paine, Robert, 71.
Parker, Lewis, 84.
Pattison, William, 64.
Paul, Isaac, 78.
Preachers, hardships, 8, 36, 44, 46; salary, 15, 45; personal appearance, 23, 44, 125; zeal to convert, 28; reprimanded, 31, 33, 44, 116; local, 37, 121; enforce law, 39, 40; practice medicine, 40; meager training, 41, 64, 66; interest in education, 43; marriage discouraged, 45, 59; in earthquake region, 51; illiterate, 65; school teachers, 69; book agents, 79; intemperate, 102, 109; agents of reform, 105, 111; expulsions, 109, 112; fight against power of bishops, 114, 119; orders of ministry, 120; total number in 1824, 127.
Presbyterians, 9; in Tennessee, 5; in Kentucky, 19; lead in education, 69, 71.
Presiding elder, duties, 119.
Quarterly Conference, plan, 116.
Quinn, James, 59.
Quitman, John A., 101.
Raikes, Robert, 73.
Ramsay, David, 100.
Ramsey, J. G. M., 7.
Rankin, John, 94.
Reelfoot Lake, 50.
Religious toleration, 13.
Rice, Daniel, 16.
Riley, Richard, 85.

Roberts, Robert R., 123.
Robertson, James, 4, 103.
Roosevelt, Theodore, 94.
Ruter, Martin, 80.
Sale, John, 58.
Scales, Nicholas D., 87.
Schools, early interest, 62; Cokesbury, 63, 66; Bethel, 63, 70; district, 64; plans, 68, 70; Augusta, 68; taught by preachers, 69; failures, 71; successes, 72; Indian, 85, 86, 87.
Sermons, 42, camp meeting, 24, 29; by Asbury, 60, 61, 66; by O'Cull, 106; by McElroy, 106; by Axley, 107, 110.
Slavery, 58; church regulations, 94, 95, 97: committee report, 123; effect on church, 124.
Smith, Daniel, 79.
Soule, Joshua, on Indians, 89; on slavery, 91, 95; bishop, 127.
Steward, duties, 121.
Stewart, John, 34, 81.
Stringfield, Thomas, 86.
Sunday schools, origin, 73; early efforts, 74; unions, 75, 78; regulations, 76; at Nashville, Tennessee, 76; growth, 78.
Talley, Alexander, 89, 125.
Tennessee, settlement, 4; constitution of 1796, 13; manumission act of 1801, 96; temperance movement, 103.
Tennessee Conference, formed, 53; of 1812, 55; of 1813, 56; of 1814, 58; of 1815, 61; plans for seminary, 71; divisions, 82, 123. 127; plans for Indian mission, 82; of 1822, 86; of 1824, 88; rules on slavery, 96, 97; of 1821, 116.
Tennessee mission, 84.
Tiffin, Edward, 9.
Tigert, John J., 3.
Tract Society, 79.
Travelers, European, 13.
Trustee, duties, 121.
Vasey, Thomas, 2.
War of 1812, moral effect, 56; economic effect, 57.
Wesley, Charles, 2.
Wesley, John, 4, conversion, 1; power of ordination, 2; on education, 62, Sunday schools, 73, 74; book room, 78; writings, 79; on slavery, 91: on whiskey, 103; autocrat, 112.
Wesleyan Female College, 72.
West, early immigration, 4; living conditions, 11, 124; scarcity of literature, 12; observance of Sabbath, 12; lack of social life, 18; rowdyism, 30, 39, 106; new lands, 60, 126; schools, 69; religious literature, 79; prevalence of whiskey, 100, 102, 105; lack of transportation, 101; contribution of local preacher, 121; extent of church, 128.

INDEX 151

Western Conference, formed, 17; of 1808, 32; increase from earthquakes, 52, 54; division, 53; slavery rule, 96.
West Tennessee, first sacrament, 83.
Whatcoat, Richard, 2, 33.
White, Hugh L., 109.
Whitefield, George, 62; on slavery, 93.
Wilberforce, William, 92.
Wilkins, Henry, 56.
Winans, William, 33.
Wyandot mission, 81.
Yale, 62.
Young, Benjamin, 31.
Young, Jacob, 101, 105.
Zion Herald, 80.